Legal Disclaimer

The author of this book is not an attorney and makes no claim to be one. The information in this book does not create or constitute a client relationship. The materials presented in this book are based solely on the experiences of the author.

Table of Contents

FORWARD

I want to thank you very much for purchasing **MS Word Legal – *Awareness Explosion*** with BONUS!. This book represents a portion of the 6 years of articles that I have contributed to various blogs. I have a secondary volume that will follow almost immediately. If you like this volume, then you will love Volume 2. Volume 2 is an array of situations that will save you hours and hours of frustrating time trying to figure out the solution. We have already been through the scenario and you will certainly appreciate the effort. These books give you a window into working in a top-tier legal word processing center. This book goes over a tremendous amount of material as well. Each article is very different from the previous and this book covers a lot of ground to say the least.

After looking at the articles produced as a whole, I realized, that so much ground has been covered that I saw the need to release it to the public. This book can be used as a study guide for people trying to get into the legal business, to increase the awareness of those working within a legal environment and to give others such as job agency people and those working for single practitioners and smaller offices, a good feel of the day to day interactions and subject matter encountered within a large law firm. I found that blogs move very fast in that an article that I write today will be way down the line and out of sight within a few days and in some cases a few hours. Nevertheless, the information that I touch upon is vital and important and through the medium of self publishing, I can reach and help an exponential amount of people.

There are a lot of technical books on the market, but few that capture the essence of this niche market and the real feel of what goes on in a law firm from day to day. If you take the time to go through the 60 or so articles that are taken from the original posts, you will surely increase your knowledge base and level of understanding without a doubt.

I write the articles I do because I see too much generic talk and wanted to make sure that people deal with and see what really goes on from day to day the good and sometimes stressful. Think of this series as a great expansion of your knowledge base.   Feel free to follow me on legaltestready.com and on Twitter @legaltestready. Through that site you can contact us for basic-advanced Legal MS Word Training. We do public training as well as transforming legal firms large and small with our style of training.

Best regards,

Louis

MS WORD LEGAL *AWARENESS EXPLOSION* Vol. 1

Articles That Increase Your Ms Word Knowledge Base

ARTICLES FROM YESTERDAY AND TODAY

I. Articles Relating to Working In A Legal Word Processing Center

It's "Normal" to Create a Style

The play on words in the title is meant as a reminder when creating a style from scratch.

If you need to create a style, you always want to start with a clean slate before you name the style and select the attributes that will make up that style.

1. To start with a clean slate, you need to have your cursor on an Empty Return that is in "**Normal**" style. You can also have your cursor within a paragraph that is within "Normal" style. If you need to strip the paragraph to "Normal" in order to do so you do **Control+Shift+N** and any formatting in that paragraph will be removed.

2. If you create a style where your cursor was sitting within let's say some "body text" style then there is no clean slate because you are starting off with a style that already has attributes that may contradict what you are trying to do with your new style so always start from scratch. Always remember that no matter where your cursor is when you are creating a style always choose "**Style Based On Normal**".

3. Don't include the automatic update feature because if you need to add direct formatting to a particular paragraph that has your new Style applied to it, you don't want that direct formatting (underscore, bolding, etc.) to now become part of the attributes of the style itself.

4. Finally, when naming your styles, make sure that they make sense not only to you but to another operator or secretary that sees that style name. They should be able to know immediately what its purpose is.

........*

Quick and Easy Deletion of a Table

This short write-up will provide you with an additional piece of knowledge that is a time saver. It has to do with the deletion of a table.

When working with tables, most people like to work in "**Print Layout View**" so that they can click on the "**Target**" symbol that appears in the top-left hand portion of the table which allows one to select the entire table with 1 click. When in **Draft View**, there is no target like symbol.

So, most people when deleting a table, select the table in 1 click and they then use their "**Delete**" key which knocks out the text of the table and leaves behind the empty grid which still leaves you with having to delete the structure of the table.

So, we can take care of the deletion of a table with a minimum of 2 clicks:

1.   Place your cursor in your table.

2.   Make sure you are in Print Layout View.

3.   Click on the **Target Symbol** (top left of table) to select the entire table in 1 click.

4.   Press your **Back Space key 1X** which will then delete the entire table text and structure.

5.   That is all you need to know!

Not A Bad Idea To Have Them Ready. Signature Blocks That Is.

We teach signature lines all of the time and believe it or not there are many strategies.

What we do see a lot in smaller firms is a typical signature block that starts at 3.0 on the ruler but in order to get there each line is filled with Tab Tab Tab Tab until they get to the location. So I thought maybe it was a good idea to touch upon some signature related info.

1. The Signature style throws the left margin to 3.0 on the ruler: Below is a "typical" style signature.

By: _____soft
      Name (soft)
      Title (Hard)

2. Above we have your typical signature block. The single line you see would have been produced using a right tab in the ruler with a solid line leader attached to the tab setting with a soft return. Name and Title would use the hanging indent to position them under the underscore.

3. Then we have those signature block situations where you have dual signature blocks and we make use of a two column table no lines with the routine I just showed up above. Remember, within a table use **control + tab** to make a tab within a cell.

4. Even when people have one column signature blocks they still opt to make use of a two column table without lines but make use of the right column only in terms of dropping in the individual signatures.

5. Knowing that the need for 2 column and 1 column signature blocks comes up often you can

A. Write a macro if you are up to it or

B. Create a document that either has a right side signature block ready to go using the "Signature style" that is always sitting in your styles pallet as a generic and throws the sig to 3.0 on the ruler or use the two column approach.

6. All you have to do is to have one signature ready to go (as shown above) and copy the signature as necessary to accommodate each needed signature. You can also set up your signature block document and save it as a template so as needed, you can go in there and grab your blank signature block ready to go using your 2 column or signature style approach.

7. Either way, having a ready to go signature block can save time especially when there may be a number of exhibits each having signatures.

8.   Important: When you set up signatures within a table use the exact same set-up as we spoke of above:

By: _____soft
        Name (soft)
        Title (Hard)

When in a table, once you have one signature the way you like it, you can simply copy the signature to the other cells of the table that need a signature. Remember that you must have a hard return after the word "Title" otherwise the signature will collapse when you attempt to copy it over to the other cells.

........*

Don't Remove Experience!

Recently I was corresponding with a student who thought that just maybe the resume was too diverse in terms of the areas of the law she was versed in and maybe the focus should be on one area alone.

I feel that each area of the law that we are exposed to helps us to grow and helps to show our all around knowledge. If during your career you have worked for a variety of attorneys who specialized in different areas such as Trademark, Corporate, Litigation, Trusts & Estates etc. this can only help.

Remember you may go to an interview let's say for a Litigation Associate or Partner and while you are there the HR person might realize you are a better fit for another open position in another area of law in that same firm. They might feel that maybe you have enough of a background to go to the center instead of just being considered for a secretarial spot alone. So you never know where your diverse experience will come into play so don't remove hard earned experience!!! For help regarding resumes, videos on going to interviews, you can go to Careerconfidential.com. You can also contact us at any time if you need help with your resume.

........*

Bablefish.com

Translation: When you need it quick but not necessarily perfect....

If you work in a WP Center then I am sure this has come up at one time or another.

Because many firms have satellite offices in different countries, you do receive requests from time to time to translate a short letter or document over to English from another language.

True story: One evening a partner comes down to the WP Center with a document in Spanish. It was a document of about 40 pages. He asked if we can get it translated to English so that he may read it. He said it does not have to be perfect, I just want to get the gist of what they were talking about. My boss at the time started calling translation services and getting quotes of $600, $ 500 for the 40 some pages of the document. They also said there would be a 48 hour turnaround.

The Partner was not happy and was protesting about can't we just get a basic translation? I decided to go up to the front and volunteered that the program Bablefish could do a page at a time and it should take about an hour or so.

My boss said to me now that you volunteered the job is now yours. So, I took one page at a time of Spanish, converted it to English and dropped it in to a new MS Word document. When I was finished with the 40 pages I emailed the final styled document to the Partner and he was very happy to say the least.

I have also had occasion to translate Japanese, Chinese and Arabic over to English to assist an attorney who needed to read the document which was not in his/her native language. It should be noted that that the Babel Fish translator comes in a few varieties. Sometimes there are links that will do a line at a time and then there are links like **systransoft.com** where they feature the Web Page at a time and a document at a time feature. I would find one you are comfortable with whether it be from Yahoo or Google, **itranslate4.eu etc.** and bookmark it and have it ready to go.

Remember this tip. Sooner or later it will come up and you will be ready!

........*

The Color White when Using Basic Shapes

This comes into play during the following scenario:

Let's say that you just finished creating cascading paragraphs on the cover page of a Preliminary Prospectus or Registration Statement. You would recognize the cascading paragraphs from their distinctive upside down triangle shape that they take on from the use of using opposing right triangle basic shapes to create them.

When they are created, the last and final step is to have the lines of the opposing right triangles to be made invisible.

1. The most common error is under formatting of the basic shapes when an individual chooses "**no color**" (used to be called "**No Line**") which causes the shapes in essence to collapse and the paragraph is no longer triangle shaped.

2. In order to allow the basic shapes to do their job but be invisible, you must use the color "white" for the lines then there is no collapse and you have your cascading text.

3. Use the color white for the lines of a basic shape for any situation where you want to allow the basic shape being used to perform its purpose while remaining invisible.

4. Red Herrings and Cascading Text are part of our class offerings and are easy to learn. Red Herrings refer to the **vertical disclaimer text** that appears in red on the cover page of a Preliminary Prospectus.

5. **As to cascading paragraphs.** When the document is saved as an MS Word 97-2003, the method seems to work fine. When saved as a "Word" (Docx) document, we then see a bleed of the text into the right side shape being used which is usually a Right Triangle and it does not go into its necessary "V" shape. The way we fix this is we select the right side "Right Triangle" and **right click**. We then go to **"Wrap Text"** and choose **"Edit Wrap Points"**. When we click on **"Edit Wrap Points"** we simply tug on the points until they lay directly on the intended shape. So, when it is done, you are looking at your Right Triangle with your "Edit Points" taking on the shape of the right side **"Right Triangle"**. Remember, at the very end to select both shapes (Click and Shift Click) and change the line color over to "White".

Below is the way it should look when it is working.

Cascading Text. - Cascading Text. - Cascading Text. - Cascading Text. - Cascading Text.
Cascading Text. - Cascading Text. - Cascading Text. - Cascading Text. - Cascading Text.
Cascading Text. - Cascading Text. - Cascading Text. - Cascading Text. - Cascading Text.
Cascading Text. - Cascading Text. - Cascading Text. - Cascading Text. - Cascading
Text. - Cascading Text. - Cascading Text. - Cascading Text. - Cascading Text.
Cascading Text. - Cascading Text. - Cascading Text. - Cascading Text.
Cascading Text. - Cascading Text. - Cascading Text. - Cascading Text.
Cascading Text. - Cascading Text. - Cascading Text. - Cascading Text. - c

........*

Some Tips for Affecting Two Basic Shapes Simultaneously:

These are tips that I used many times when dealing with shapes when doing cascading text. But, it does not matter, they are useful for any shapes you are working with.

1. First if you need to quickly dupe a shape you can use **Control D.** That will immediately produce a **duplicate** shape. If you are duping the shape for purposes of doing Cascading Text (meaning you are using right triangles) then you are going to need to use the flip horizontal feature so that you make sure that the second triangle is facing in towards the first right triangle.

2. Whether you are using right triangles or not and wish to affect both of the shapes **"simultaneously"** so that making a shape larger, smaller, wider, narrower the two shapes will respond exactly the same you do the following:

A. **Click** on the first shape **1 time**

B. Go to the second shape and do **Shift Click**

C. Now whatever you do will affect both shapes simultaneously.

D. **Micro Moving** shapes is easy as well. If you need to nudge a shape into place whether it is a text box, (red herring), lines, arrows, ovals etc. you click twice on the shape and using your **control** and **directional arrow** keys you can micro move the object into place. Up, down, left, right. Give it a try.

........*

Structure First: Then Style The Document.

Whether at work or about to take a Legal WP Test, you want to learn to look at a document in entirety so that you have a game plan.

So if you are given an assignment at work or about to take a test that involves constructing let us say a large litigation document from scratch, then you need a plan that makes the process a smooth one. Consider the following for a routine:

1. Examine the Entire document. Is there a TOC, TOA, Index of Terms?

2. Are there Exhibits?

3. Is there a multi-level outline?

4. Is there a caption box? What style of Caption Box.

5. Look at the numbering system

So after a good look I would:

1. Create a Cover Page. Vertical Align Center. Check if you need to do a Page Border on your Cover Page.

2. Create Separate Pages for your TOC, TOA, Index of Terms. Make sure you have a section break after your Index of Terms to separate from the main part of the document. Make sure your numbering is Romanette style (i, ii, iii...) for these pages.

3. Establish your page numbering for the main part of your document but do not number the first page of the main part of the document. The numbering style is 1,2,3,4, etc. Make sure that different first page under Page Layout, Page Set-up and Layout is set for Section Break, New Page, Different First Page.

4. Establish a separate section in the back of the document for each individual Exhibit with the Exhibit page number set-up. The numbering set-up should be A-1, B-1, C-1 etc.

Once this entire structure is set up now you can style the document and mark it appropriately for the TOA and Index of Terms. You will use your Heading Styles for the levels of your Multi-Level Outline.

When you are finished with the outline and styling process then everything is already set up as to the running of the TOC, TOA and Index of Terms.

If you take care of the structure first, then your time spent will be that much more efficient.

........*

Hard Space

Hard Space, Non-Breaking Space and Required Space.

All of the items listed in the heading of this write-up all pertain to the same thing. but, in the center, it is most commonly referred to as the Hard Space.

For the most part, many operators and secretaries don't use it or forgot to use it. A Hard Space also known as Required Space as well as Non-breaking Space simply serves to keep two items together such as John Q Smith. A hard space would be placed between the John and Q so that the Q does not separate from John and wrap around to the next line leaving the name John at the end of the line by itself. Another example is January 1, 2013. We would place the hard space between the January and the 1 so that January 1 does not separate but acts like one piece of text.

Another very common use of the Hard Space is when you have numbering all throughout a paragraph whether it is (1), (i), (a), (l) etc.

And another example:

Creditors. The Company received approval for the meeting which was chaired by a Company Director. Scheme Creditors admitted to vote, voted in favor of the Scheme. The Court noted, among other things, the following with respect to the votes: (1) one of the largest claimants had no Very Untrue Claim, (2) two creditors who had Accrued Claims and Very Untrue Claims voted their unsplit claims in full; (3) 16 of the 34 reinsureds who voted in favor of the Scheme were also reinsures of the Company; (4) the majority of reinsureds had no or only modest Untrue Claims; ¶

If you notice within the **example above**, there are four sentences that are numbered. Also note that after each closed parenthesis, is followed by a word that we do not want to have separate from the closed parenthesis. The hard space that we will place between the closed parenthesis and the word that follows serves to make sure that the number such as (1) and the word following **never separate** so that the number (1) is not left at the end of the line and the word following goes to the next line. That is to say that the (1) and the word that follows stay together as **one piece.** .

Inserting Hard Spaces as Needed.

In order to make the Hard Space first make sure that there are no regular spaces between the two items that you wish to have stay as one piece.

1. Place the cursor between the two items and do **Control + Shift** and tap the Space Bar **1X.**

2. There should be only the hard space between the two items. If there is a **hard space** and a **regular space** it not work.! When you insert a hard space it produces a degree like symbol °.

What if there are many Instances of Items Needing Hard Space and time is of the Essence?

Many times while working on a document in the center, you see paragraph after paragraph that needs hard space protection. Well if you are in a position where an attorney is pressing the Coordinator to get the job back, you obviously are not going to be picking through a document looking for hard spaces to insert.

There are two things you can do in this situation.

1. After you have done all of your edits, look through the document keeping your focus on the right side of the page. You are looking for stragglers that are by themselves at the end of a line that are in need of a hard space.

2. You can also do a **global replace** if you so desire in order to take care of all hard space situations at one time. In order to do so do the following:

A, Do **Control H.** This brings up your **Find and Replace** Dialog Box

B. In the **Find What** area type in a **Closed Parenthesis** and a regular space

C. In the **Replace with** area put in a Closed Parenthesis and Click the "More" Button followed by the "Special" Button and select Non-Breaking Space.

D. Select Replace All and all of the areas in need of hard space protection should now be done. You may wish to highlight a paragraph at a time or a number of paragraphs at a time and run the replace. **Having the paragraph(s) highlighted will force the "Replace" function to stop,** tell you how many instances have been replaced and thus giving you the ability to go forward and/or stop the global replace as needed.

........*

Picking up a Job from another Operator or Secretary:

Many of you will leave unfinished work to be picked up by another operator for completion while some of you will be the recipient of this work. The person who leaves the works truly affects the outcome by how clear they are in their turnover instructions. So here is a good reminder of those considerations:

Whether you are picking up a job from a secretary or another operator the thing that you do not want to happen is when the information concerning the job is incomplete or too general.

For example:

You come to work and waiting just for you is a very heavy mark-up 80-100 pages. There is heavy editing on the hard copy itself, (both front and back) many riders in the form of hand written text, requests for info to be inserted in from other documents to the present doc, and pieces of hard copy that are labeled as rider material to be keyed in at various locations in the main document.

What are we looking for on this pick-up sheet or however the firm handles the passing of an incomplete job to another secretary or WP operator?

1. A **clear instruction** on where to pick up. Please don't just leave the note: "search for bookmark called pickup". What if it did not take? That means I may have to call you at home and pray that you pick up or waste time trying to figure out your actual pick-up point.

2. Have you been doing the **riders** as you were editing or were you saving them for last? Were the large **hard copy riders** already **scanned in** and OCR'd so that I don't have to key them in from scratch? If so, what operator worked on them and what are the document numbers associated with these rider documents?

3. Are there items needing to be marked such as **TOA** or **Index of Terms**.

4. If there is not a control sheet was there an initial request to make a **new version** or **dupe the document** before editing?

5. Once the editing is done, are there clear instructions for who to email the document to, provide a redline of the document, print out the document, hold the hard copy or inter office it back? All these things have to be known.

6. It is not lost on me that at the end of a shift, people are tired and want to go home but a rush job in terms of handing off an incomplete job is a recipe for trouble. Stop your work 15 minutes before you have to leave and produce a clean turnover set of instructions. Believe me, your reputation will go way up if you consistently provide a clear and smooth handoff to the next person continuing the job you were working on.

PDF Files From The DeskTop vs. Scanned Files

This is an important subject.

1. First things first. If you PDF a document such as a MS Word File while you are in MS Word it is referred to as "**from the desktop**". The resulting PDF is clean and **immediately** searchable. You will also be able to lift text and copy it to other documents (unless you put security on) as insert or rider information. You would of course make use of paste special when bringing the text into the target document.

2. Then there are PDF files resulting from scanning a paper copy and saving it as a PDF. The resulting PDF is in essence a document of static pictures each picture representing a single page of the PDF file. In order to make that text searchable you run the **Recognize Text Feature** in Adobe Professional. Those of you that have an older version of Adobe Professional (Version 6 or lower) you use **Paper Capture**. In order for the text to be recognized you would have had to scan the document in at a minimum of **300 DPI** or else the recognize text feature will not work.

3. Once Recognize text is complete, you will be able to search the PDF file as well as lift text from it as well.

4. It should be noted that as it relates to paper copies being scanned, your results will heavily depend upon the quality and condition of the paper copy that was used when it was originally scanned. Always seek the best possible paper copy before scanning. It should be clean and the text should be clear not blurry as would be the case with a copy of a copy of a copy....

5. To **truly protect** PDF content. In your word document or PDF file make a watermark. Make sure it is not too light and not too dark.

6. Print out the document with the watermark. Now scan the paper copy with the watermark and save as a PDF at a setting less than 300 DPI. If they try to run the recognize text feature it will not work and if they run it through the scanner again the watermark will interrupt the process and if you attempt to lift the text it will be a jumbled mess. They would be forced to key everything in from scratch. So, if someone is going to attempt to lift text of a PDF that sensitive work or copyright work you might as well make it as labor intensive on them as possible.

Changing The Normal.Doc or Normal.Docm Template

Premise: Every time I create a new document, I don't have the Font that I use the majority of the time, my before and after spacing that I use is not there as well, the alignment of the paragraphs and the basic body text styles that I wish to have available for instant use each time I create a new file is not available in my new document either.

So, what is the **normal.dot** or **normal.dotm**? This is the "blank" document shell on which all new MS Word documents that you personally create are based.

1. In 2003 and below, we called this the **Normal.Dot** Template. In 2007 and above, they call it **Normal.Dotm**. The "m" stands for **macro enabled**. Either way, whatever is in this document template in terms of settings and/or styles will be what is immediately available each time you create a new document.

2. If you work in a large firm then they have standardized the Normal.Dotm with the "**Firm**" settings including the "**Firm**" styles. If at a larger firm your Normal.Docm template has become corrupted or is missing things, the IT Department will simply refresh the file so you are back in business and all intended settings and styles are restored.

3. At home or in a smaller firm do the following in order to affect your main document template (Normal.DotM)

4. To Get To The Template:

Open MS Word.

In 2007, click on the Office Button in the upper left corner of your screen. Click on **Open**. Under Microsoft Office Word there will be a folder labeled **Templates**. Click **Templates** and then double click the **Normal.dotm** file. This should open the MS Word 2007 template.

5. In 2010, click **File**> **Open**. Under Microsoft Word there will be a folder labeled **Templates**. Click **Templates** and then double click the **Normal.dotm** file. This should open the MS Word 2010 template.

6. Press < **Ctrl + a** > on the keyboard to select everything (even though there is nothing but one blank line there). Now you are free to change the Font (perhaps to Times New Roman), and Font Size (perhaps to 12), the body text styles you want to have available, the before and after spacing, the margins, different first page, field shading always, style area width for draft view etc. etc.

7. Save the document template with your changes. All **future** documents created will now reflect the changes you just made. You can always go back and amend this template as needed.

In Word 2007 and above, in the **Developer** tab, choose **Document Template** and then click on **Organizer**. If you don't see the **Developer** tab, then click Office®Word Options®Popular, and click to enable Show Developer tab in the ribbon. Once there, the Organizer is pretty self-explanatory. Once in the Organizer the Normal.dotm file will be represented on the right side of the Organizer.

........*

Relative vs. Absolute

It comes up all the time. This concept of **relative vs. absolute** has been present in the earliest word processing programs to the latest MS Word Software.

Once in a while it will come up on a test and if you don't know what it refers to right off the bat well we will solve that in this short write-up.

Example No. 1

1. You are going along with your document and at a specific location you now have the need to turn the page orientation to landscape. If you have used a center tab (upside down T) in the ruler then you will notice that your page numbering is off and is no longer centered and must be repositioned on the ruler (dragged to the right) in order to make sure that the page numbering sits neatly centered in the landscape portion of the document. This is an example of **Absolute**. It is where it is and you need to take action to reposition the tab.

2. If you had made use of the center icon then when you turned your page to landscape the page numbering would simply automatically reposition itself and therefore thus a good example of **Relative**. Center is center. In this case, Relative means no matter what the page width it will center the numbering.

3. One more example. You bring in a picture. You right click and go to format picture. You wish to manipulate the size of the picture.

4. You click on **Lock Aspect Ratio**.

As you change the **height** the **width** automatically adjusts. This is an example of a **Relative** response.

5. You unclick "**Lock Aspect Ratio**" and when you change the height, the width does **Not** auto adjust. This is an example of an absolute response.

6. You should now be more comfortable with these two terms. Can you think of more examples?

Kindle Interesting:

Recently I had to upload a book to Kindle for an attorney. It was a good experience because I believe many of you will at some point be doing it soon as more attorneys realize that they can publish their own books without a hassle. The document itself was an MS Word document. In order to upload the book for optimum quality you had to know a few things:

1. All pictures had to be brought into the document as a JPEG.

2. The Chapter Headings for the TOC used Heading 1 only

3. The margins were 1.5 left and right with 12Pts. after

4. I had to save the document as an **Web Page Filtered** document which does the following: It converts the file to an HTML file and then creates a separate folder with all of your pictures that had been used in the book.

5. You then go to the HTML file and make it a zip file and you then go to the picture folder and drag the entire folder into the zip file as well.

6. It is **this zip folder** containing the **HTML file** and the **folder of photos** that gets uploaded to the Kindle system. Your cover page for the book is not part of the actual book file and is uploaded separately before the book is uploaded. The cover page is a **JPEG**. If you want a thorough book on preparing and publishing you can go to Kindle, Barnes and Nobel or Kobo and Search for the book Low Cost Empire Volume 3, Creating An Industry From Your Book. This will teach you how to create a book from scratch and monetize it as well.

7. Once your book is uploaded to Kindle, it is available for purchase between 12 and 24 hours.

........*

Crowding of the Number System on the Table of Contents or Table of Authorities as well as Proper Font for Headings within Table of Contents and Table of Authorities.

There are **two issues** here that I wish to examine. If you look a typical Table of Authorities and you look at the Heading (Cases) with a style associated with it of "**TOA Heading**" you will notice that the individual **Cases** listed in the TOA are usually in Times New Roman 12 while the **TOA Heading** may not be. Sometimes this heading defaults to Ariel 12 which is a common quirk of the system. Most operators don't even notice it and routinely hand in work where the fonts of the document are not uniform. So, in order to **fix the TOA Heading** you can either Double click on the TOA Heading style listed on the left hand side in **draft view** or **right click** on the TOA Heading style within the **Formatting Panel** on the **Right hand side style pallet**. If you place your cursor on the "**Cases**" Line the **TOA Heading style** name will appear in the top window of the side Panel. I will use that side panel method to correct the style.

1. Right Click on TOA Heading.

2. Under Modify, change the Font over to Times New Roman. If you do it through **Modify** then the fix is permanent. If you do it through **direct formatting** then every time that someone runs the Table of Authorities (Updates it) it will simply go back to the way it was before it was fixed since it was not corrected within the actual style but on the surface due to direct formatting.

NEXT ISSUE:

Take a look at a typical TOA. Now I want to focus on the text that sometimes crowds the page numbers to the extreme right. This is a sloppy look and most often an attorney will spot it and ask for it to be corrected. Many people do not know how to do this properly so they manually go to the ruler and fix it like that. But, each time that the TOA is updated the problem resurfaces since it was done with direct formatting. . So, the question becomes **what controls the text of the completed TOA** so that we can improve the look of the TOA and it will be fixed once and for all.

Look at the left hand side of a completed TOA in draft view. The style associated with the completed TOA entries is called "**Table of Authorities**". I want you to do the following:

1. Either **double click** on the left hand side style "Table of Authorities" or **right click** on the right hand side panel where it says the name of the style "Table of Authorities".

2. Under **Modify**, go to Format Paragraph and under Indentation "**Right**" make that **0.5**. That will take all of the text of the Table of Authorities and will push it back towards the left an additional 0.5 **thus making a clear lane** between the Table of Authorities Text and the Page Numbering.

3. If you look at the **ruler** when your cursor is in the TOA you will notice that there is a right tab in the ruler toward the extreme right. You **DO NOT TOUCH THAT**. The right tab controls the actual **Page numbering** all the way to the **right**.

4. Finally it is very important to note that if your **Table of Contents** has this problem of crowding, you will go about fixing it in the same manner by modifying the styles **TOC 1** and **TOC 2** which are the styles associated with a completed Table of Contents.

........*

The Basics of Doing Tables In A Legal Environment

In a Word Processing Legal Center, if you have experienced it, you then know that there is a routine for every possible move you make. One thing that draws attention good and bad, are financial tables. Being a coordinator for many years, one hears all of the disgruntled comments and under the breath mumbling of operators undoing something that they perceive done improperly.

Many times it is the financial tables within a legal document. So, let's go over some basics.

1. First, when first creating the table, select the table and remove the **border lines**, remove **before and after spacing**, make sure that the "Cell" alignment is **Bottom** and while the entire table is highlighted decide upon a Font Size. Font size will come

into play if you have many columns to deal with and you are using a Portrait set-up. Depending on the Table you may wish to **center** the table **horizontally** on the page.

2. Next, for the cells that will contain numbers, make sure they are all in Left Alignment.

3. For lines where numbers use a $ sign you place a right tab in the ruler in a position on the ruler that will allow the numbers to come in neatly under the main headings.

4. For lines where numbers DO NOT use a $ sign we place a "**Decimal Align**" tab in the ruler in a position that will allow the numbers to come in and line up neatly under the $ sign lines.

5. For lines that use **single or double underscore**, always use the **paragraph** choice under **Borders and Shading**. This will leave a minute amount of space on the left and right side of the cell so there is a clear delineation between the cells of different columns rather than underscore lines appearing to be one long line.

6. Using these simple instructions above will help you to be more on target when you are dealing with Financial Tables within a legal environment.

........*

Footnote Ref. vs. Footnote Text

Footnote Ref/Footnote Text

This is considered a minor item in the scheme of things. It comes down to if you are asked to modify Footnotes in terms of their **Reference Numbers** vs. the actual **Footnote text** you can waste time figuring it out if you don't know it right off the bat. You can use **Control Shift S** (Apply Styles Tool Bar) in order to quickly and easily see the styles that your cursor is presently sitting on.

You need to know how to modify the actual styles that represent the **Footnote numbers** vs. the **Footnotes Text**.

1. You might be in a situation whereby the attorney wanted for whatever reason wants an alteration to the size or look of the text. Typically, law firms use Times New Roman 12 for the bulk of the document and the Footnotes are done **two point sizes down** which gives you **Times New Roman 10**.

2. When you insert a Footnote, you end up with a footnote number or a footnote symbol depending on what you choose for the numbering system. You have a Footnote Reference Number within the body of the text which appears **Superscripted** as well as a **corresponding Reference number** at the bottom of the page associated with the new footnote.

3. If you sweep your cursor over the **footnote reference number** "within the text" and look up to your style window or your style task pane to the right, you will see that it reads "**Footnote Reference**". Keep in mind that this is a character style "**a**" and is not a paragraph style. Therefore, you can (and would only need to) modify its font characteristics and attributes if needed such as bolding, font and font size.. This is the name of the style that is associated with the footnote number or symbol.

4. Now, if you go into print layout and run your cursor over the footnote reference number next to the actual footnote text (at the bottom of your page) the style associated with the footnote number is again "**Footnote Reference**". If you are to highlight **the text of the footnote itself** and look at your task pane, you will see that the style associated with the footnote text is called "**Footnote Text**".

5. This is important because if you should have the need to modify the footnote reference numbers or the footnote text in any way, you would know what styles control which parts of the footnote!

6. Remember, the footnote text tends to be two points below the font of the text of the document. So, if your document is in Times New Roman 12 (a very popular law firm font) then your footnotes should be in Times New Roman 10.

........*

Heading Styles and Keep with Next

We use "**Keep With Next**" when we want to prevent a particular heading from being at the bottom of the page while the paragraph that follows has separated from the Heading and now appears by itself at the top of the **next page** forward.

We also build "Keep With Next" into the heading styles when doing a document with Multi-Level Paragraph Numbering. The issue of this write-up occurs when there is an overuse of "**Keep With Next**" where it is built into all or most of the Heading levels of the Multi-Level Outline. Normally, we build it into **Heading 1 and Heading 2** and then if there is a need to use the "Keep With Next" for individual situations that might occur in the other levels, we usually take care of them one by one with direct formatting.. This means applying "Keep With Next" as needed directly and not building it into Heading Levels 3 and 4 for example.

When "Keep With Next" is built into too many levels, the document starts to have trouble in terms of system page breaks. Some pages end way too early and leave large gaps on particular pages. . This is due to the fact that the document has a situation where the "Keep With Next" is acting like a large block of text that does not have the ability to do its page breaks naturally because in effect it is acting like one large glued together block.

So it is better to use the "Keep With Next" **on the first two levels of your multi-level outline document** only and take care of the situations that occur in the remaining level Headings 3,4,5 etc. with direct formatting.

........*

Using the same information for both the Merge Letters and the Labels to be printed.

In a Legal WP Center one of the more mundane chores is to do a merge "rejection letter" for the hundreds of legal professionals that send their resumes to a top-tier law firm or for that matter any size law firm. The firm responds with a friendly and kind rejection letter. It is the job of the WP Center to take care of the hundreds of letters that need to be responded to. So, some tips:

1. Set up your Main Letter. It will most probably be supplied to you.

2. Set up your secondary document. This is the document that will contain your Name and Address and Salutation information.

3. The secondary document will be composed of a two column table. The top row will have the following: The first cell of the first row will have the word **Salutation** and the first cell of the Second Row will have the word **Address** and will be composed of the Name and Address of the recipient.

4. Those two top rows will serve as the field codes in the main letter and will act as targets as to the location where the info will be plugged in. The remaining rows of your table will be for the actual info and each row of information will represent 1 recipient.

5. After you run the merge and your letters are ready you will need to do labels for the envelopes. When you run the merge for envelopes, you only need to use your **"address"** field code and your names and addresses are already done and waiting for you since you had already keyed that info in preparing the letters.

6. For return address labels use the 80 to a sheet labels and type in the info 1x and copy that info to all 80 labels. Then, for each sheet you print, you will have 80 return labels at your disposal.

I wrote a great book on Merge For Law Firms and you can get it on **www.lowcostempire.com** and look for MS Word Business.

........*

Pick One and Stick To It

When working in a WP Center, it is common to come across Litigation Documents containing Table of Authorities Entries that are mixed. Some of the TOA entries are underscored while others are italic. The underscore or the italic should end after the plaintiff and defendant are identified.

Most of the time the mixture is due to copying text in from other sources whereby the other sources are already using one or the other.

Some things you should know:

1. The attorney or paralegal will determine whether you underscore or italicize the Table of Authorities entries in the body of the text.

2. Once that decision is made, comb through the document and look for inconsistencies.

3. If you are fortunate enough to have a proofreader on board, alert them to look for stragglers so that the document is consistent all the way through.

4. Alert the secretary for that attorney to be aware of same.

5. Run the TOA and submit it back to the attorney for review and/or further editing.

........*

Making Good Use of Section Printing

This feature has come to the rescue many a time when the pressure is on, an attorney is standing in the center with you or at your secretarial station, he/she is pacing back and forth and they need a particular piece of a large document right away.

Some of you know exactly what I am referring to. They want a particular piece of the document printed because they need to edit it, they need to go to a meeting with it, they have a conference call due to come in and they just need a particular piece of the whole: What are some of those things that people do and what can you do?

1. An initial thing people do under pressure is to send the entire document to print. Then they look for the piece that is requested while the attorney looks at them like they are crazy.

2. Misinterpret the page numbering system within the document 1,2,3 (the page numbering assigned to a particular portion of the document) etc. vs. Page 4 of 120 meaning the "system page count" for that document. This usually results in (over or under printing) pieces or parts of the document that were not requested.

3. If you are familiar with the document to an extent, then a particular exhibit will have its own section, the main part of the document, will have its own section, the cover page that is vertical aligned center will have its own section, (if you have a cover page) the TOC, TOA, Index of terms depending on the length, will have it own section or individual sections, a portion of the document that has a wide financial

table that needed to be placed in the document in landscape will have its own section. Get it?

4. Knowing this when you go to print, you can select for example print S-5 which means print the 5th section of the document which may be a particular exhibit or print S-3 which may be the main part of the document or S-4 which may be that wide financial table so you use this as a way to target a piece within a large file.

Play with this the next time you have a large file. Keep this in the forefront and it will help you to be more efficient in certain situations.

Line Numbering Stemming from the Header.

This is one of those requests that crop up once in a while but if it is you who needs to deal with it, you will surely want to know how.

The situation: Line numbering places a number next to each line whether we are using single or double space. When we use line numbering, anytime that it comes across a table, there will be a gap in the line numbering until it gets past the table. Upon coming across plain text, it will again start to number picking up where it left off. Here is the problem: Some attorneys do not like the gaps as it pertains to how line numbering omits numbering when coming across tables. They want uniformity meaning line numbering from top to bottom on every page.

They want every page to be uniform so that for example every page has the numbers 1-25 page after page and all pages look the same uninterrupted no matter what is going on that page. So, in order to get around this problem that exists when using traditional line numbering, we will insert our own line numbering that will be consistent on every page no matter whether there is text or tables.

So, how do we go about setting this up?

1. Open up your Header on Page 1 of the main part of the document.

2. Create a Text Box while the Header is open

3. Right Click on the text box and under Format, size it approximately 8.50 - 9.00 inches long and 0.40 wide.

4. Position the empty text box to the edge of the **first instance of text on page 1** where the **No. 1** in your text box will be. You can use the Control **Key and the Directional Arrows for micro moving of the text box** if need be. Note:: once your Header is **open** you can position the text box with the numbers anywhere you need to. It (the text box) will **always be associated with the Header** regardless of where you position the text box. You may need to copy the completed text box to the next header in the same section if using the Different First Page Option.

5. I am going to assume that **you are using double spacing for the paragraphs of the document.** Go into the text box and type 1-25 and/or 1-27 with a hard return after each number. I say 1-25 or 27 because you may have variations with your top and bottom margins. Let us also assume that we are using 1 inch top and bottom.

After you type in the numbers, highlight the contents of the text box by clicking inside the text box and doing **Control A.** Format the text box to have 12 Pts. after each number. Yes the text box should be using single space but 12 Pts. After. Also, choose Right Alignment for the numbers in the text box.

6. In my opinion, this method works best for Double Spaced documents. The line numbering should go up until right before the Footer area.

7. Last step is to remove the Lines of the Text Box. Right click on the border of the box and in the Format Text Box Dialog Box go to lines and select "**No Color**"

8. Make sure that your text box that stems from the Header, repeats on each and every page so that the numbering acts as a template and every page has uninterrupted line numbering throughout the entire main portion of the document.

9. Three things: if you have a cover page, TOC, TOA, Index of Terms then you do not have to start the line numbering until the **first page of the actual document.** Some people might say, why don't you just use pre-lined paper? You can, but pre-lined usually has a double red line after the numbers, you may not have numbered paper available and you may not have enough time to make a template type page to make your own pre-numbered paper.

Finally if you wish to make the page more aesthetically pleasing, you can do a page border that only uses the left and right (no top or bottom) where you place a double line on the left where the numbers will line up and a single line on the right for a more traditional look.

........*

Where Did My Section Counter Go?

A couple of weeks ago, I gave you a scenario of having to print out specific sections of a document to avoid having to print everything but a lot of people get frustrated when having to do so because in MS Word 2003 it was a given. The Section was always at the bottom left. so all we had to do was to find the area of the large document and see what section it resides in and print that section.

It was always at the bottom of your screen and any time you needed to know what section you were in, you simply looked at your status at the bottom. For whatever reason, it is no longer the default to have the section of the document you are currently in displayed at the bottom.

So if you want that classic look of the Page Number, Formatted Page Number and Section you should:

1. Right click on your status bar and you will get a laundry list of those items that can be displayed and take note that the top three are **Page Number, Formatted Page Number** and **Section**.

2. Make sure that all three are checked.

3. Formatted Page Number refers to the numbering systems that you set up within each section opposed to Page Number which is the actual page within the document regardless of how you are numbering it such as "Page 4" meaning the fourth actual page of the file regardless of the fact that it may be numbered as Page 2 by you.

So this should help a bit in restoring a piece of information that we were all used to seeing and took for granted.

........*

On the Subject Of Labels (Return Address That Is)

I am talking about the Avery 8167 which gives you 80 Labels to a sheet and the dimensions are

Height 0.5

Width. 1.75

Let us say we are using a 6 or 7 Pt. font size to accommodate this

The reason I bring this up is the way I have observed people put a sheet of Return Address together.

1. They start out by typing in the first label.

2. Then they copy it and proceed to Control V (paste) for each of the remaining 79 labels.

3. This is what you may wish to do. Put in the person's name and do a soft return (shift enter)

4. Put in the street address and put in a soft return

5. Then put in the State, City and Zip and do not do any return - soft return or hard return.

6. The State, City and Zip will be on a line that has the table cell return. Now you have your first return address

7. Highlight the first address and **do not** highlight the table cell return that appears right after the zip code and now do "Control C".

8. Hover over the first column until you get a **black arrow pointing down** and do **Control V.**

9. Highlight over the 2, 3 and fourth column individually (not all at once) where you will receive the black arrow pointing down and do Control V. Your four label columns should now be completely filled in and ready to go with your return address labels.

10. The reason that I said one column at a time instead of attempting to do all four is because in between **each column** is a **buffer column** and you do not want to disturb them so you do a column at a time but that certainly beats doing "Control V" (Paste) 79 times. The buffer columns ensure that the label columns are spaced properly. If you need 10 sheets worth of labels send the 1 page to print with 10 copies and you are done.

........*

Thumb Drives - Back Them Up

Just a few years ago, the thumb drive was an amazing development in portability. Now we have "cloud" storage and apps that let us have access to your personal documents as well as the attorneys now having access to their documents and the contents of their red-weld files as well. But the thumb drive is still very much in use and a couple of thoughts:

1. If an attorney has you place documents on a thumb drive for him/her to take with them, make sure you have a back up. In large firms, they may have a folder that is used by the WP Center on the Network where you can store a copy of what you had placed on the thumb drive. If the thumb is lost or damaged, it is not a total loss. Even if you work in a smaller firm, you can certainly make a folder on your desktop and label it back- up thumb drive.

2. What about your own thumb drive? Now, many people use their own thumb drive because they might have personal letters and personal info that they just don't feel comfortable about placing on the network of their work place. As to thumb drives in a large firm: I personally would limit their use to a minimum. Smaller firms allow you to wear many hats and allow you to be more a part of the team in a much more integral way. Therefore, they really are not going to look at you twice if you have your own thumb drive. Large firms on the other hand clearly are more security conscious; have people watching the network 24/7 and you are under a different type of scrutiny. Your role is "tightly" defined and some people (your own co-workers) will watch everything you do. Point being, even if you are innocently just using the thumb drive for your own harmless reasons other people are watching you. "Oooh, maybe that one is taking documents from the firm", and on and on. Large firms are notorious for gossip, people watching other people's movements so use discretion.

3. Finally, if you are using a thumb drive on behalf of your own attorney you work for or using your own personal thumb drive keep track of where it is at all times. I cannot tell you how many times I have found people's thumb drives still in the computer and then removed it and held it for them. Louis is honest, but I don't have to tell you how many people will simply take it and now, they have a piece of your life that they should not have so you might consider using a thumb drive that you can place on your keychain. Also, if you are sharing a work station as in a WP center, you have to be very aware of all personal belongings. Very different from sitting in a Secy cluster where no one else should be hanging around your desk and they stand out when they do.

4. Finally, if it is the thumb drive of your attorney, you really don't want to lose that. That can cause trust issues and makes you look like someone who is not focused. So, remember information that is portable comes with a responsibility so always keep that in mind whether it is for personal or professional use.

........*

Using Skype and Free Conference Call Some Thoughts and Strategy:

For the attorney. I use both on a regular basis. For free conference call, the service is great. If you join the International version, you have access to a listing of about 35 countries that your foreign clients can dial into locally. So you dial in to the US number, they dial in to their country number and both of you use the **same participant access code**.

If you are the host, you can dial in with the host access code then make use of the features such as record, mute, and other nice features. They also have a free version for screen sharing whereby you are on a conference call and someone is giving a Power Point presentation that many people are watching so this service has really developed.

One thing to remember. If you are to arrange a conference call, remember to not allow someone to have their way and have you use their free conference call number instead. If your contacts are all new to this individual, they won't be your exclusive contacts for long. Free Conference Call gives a detailed report of every participant and their phone numbers to the host. So, if you do not wish to be bypassed on your deals, do not give up your right to head the conference call with your number!

Okay, Skype is very good in letting you make free calls to anyone in the world and I do! I like to use the texting feature more because as a routine, I will use those transcripts to email to my clients and or business partners to memorialize a conversation I had. Sometimes I will first edit the transcript before sending it out in order to protect contact info from people who I have not built a solid relationship with as of yet. Many a morning, I have Skype messages waiting for me from Hong Kong, mainland China London, and other people in other countries all over the world. Skype is a cost effective way to conduct world wide business operations, communications and conference calls. But I would add that Skype has a more personal touch whereby Free Conference Call has more of a strictly business feel.

It does not matter where you reside. I would make use of both. Remember free conference call has 99 slots for a free cc so make good use of it for meetings, commercials, questions and answers and many other informational events and if the event went well and you used the record feature you can leverage the recording to play to other audiences as well thus duplicating yourself effectively while getting your message out.

........*

Vacation - Business Still Goes On

Summertime Subjects:

What is this about?

Boss goes on vacation. Business Opportunity arises for client. Boss is the liaison for bank that can do the deal. Boss is on vacation in Europe. His cell phone does not work. Associate does not know about this particular deal and is not in position to remedy the situation as well.

Client is frustrated. Secretary emails Boss and has to wait for response. Boss does not check email until later that night and opportunity has passed.

Some remedies for vacationing decision makers:

1. Before they leave. Who is filling in just in case client has work or unexpected development? Is a Partner available as well as an Associate to handle the unexpected in their place while gone.

2. What is the communication situation. Do you have the itinerary, hotel, room?

3. If not, does your boss have Skype in his/her phone. That is like having a walkie talkie. If you text a phone with Skype or ring a phone with Skype either way no matter where they are on Earth your name comes up and you can talk immediately.

4. Is his/her cell equipped with a document viewer such as PowerDocs that would allow them to immediately view Documents from email? If not, is there an Internet Cafe where they are staying or does the hotel have any facilities to assist in printing out and/or faxing documents. Do you have the electric signature of your boss and are you authorized to sign with it?

5. High level business is a responsibility, so vacation or not, things happen and you need to make sure you have covered the bases in knowing how to contact your boss in an important unexpected situation.

6. If you take these proactive type steps you will always be better off than having no solutions and looking unprepared.

........*

Checklist For Moving Operations Elsewhere

Well, you would be surprised how often there is a trial and an attorney group needs WP services or Secretarial services and Paralegals to come with them and assist them throughout the course of the trial. Sometimes, these trials can last weeks. In large firms, and it is the IT Departments job to set up the office away from the office. But, in my experience, it is really the WP people who should be consulted. Here is a checklist for an office away from the office that can function effectively.

1. Regular PC's with real keyboards not laptops. You can type a lot faster with a PC Keyboard. If you do get stuck with a laptop, you should have a mouse. unless you are really used to not using a mouse this situation is not the time to learn.

2. Supplies: paper, labels, binder clips, pens, blank CD's, thumb drives, envelopes of all sizes.

3. A listing of all attorney numbers and extensions where they can be reached if their firm numbers have not been forwarded. Cell phone numbers as well. Firm listing of all attorney email and numbers should also be included as well as international satellite offices.

4. Internet lines that have been tested and are in working order including firm email system.

5. Laser printers with extra toner for the proper printer.

6. A small copier.

7. Numbers for international conference calls ready to go. Numbers for Fed Ex and DHL, Car companies for rides as well as package delivery.

8. Finally, think about little things that are often overlooked. A true story: Once, we had a trial in Tel Aviv Israel. They shipped all of the equipment from the New York office to Israel. When they set up the temporary location and plugged in

equipment it burnt out and smoked and nothing could be worked on because they did not account for AC current vs. DC current. Then the frenzy for adapters took over. Thinking out a move like this takes a little time. If done correctly, will make it a smooth process overall.

........*

Perhaps you've had experience of my question which was How best to work with documents that pass between firms?

Okay here is my take on the subject:

1. A lot of this issue has to do with time. Just because something comes in from the outside does not mean that you strip the document right off the bat. What if the attorney says I just sent you a document in the email. I need you to get it on the system right away and get it to me. Well, I cannot tell you how many times some very uptight operator said "'our policy is to strip everything coming from the outside immediately." My policy is to take the attorney at his word. If he asked for the document right away, I assume he needs it for some reason either to search the file for some info or to scoop up text and place into another document. What you could do in this situation before you place it on the system is to first save it on your hard drive.

2. Go into MS Word and do File open, search for the file on the hard drive and click on the document name 1x.

3. On the "Open" button there is an arrow to the right. Click on the arrow and choose "**open and repair**". It will open the document and for the most part knock out any minor corruption within the document. Then go ahead and place the document on the system and get it to the attorney as requested.

4. You can always ask the attorney whether he wants the document stripped and firm styled overnight. He will either say not necessary or yes please do so.

5. When you do an old fashion strip of a document that came in from the outside you essentially want to lift the text out of the existing shell and place it in a new shell.

6. So in the document from another firm go to the top Control Home. Press F8 (extended highlighting). Press Control + End which takes you to the end of the document and highlights everything along the way but does not include the Visual Basic info from the original shell as control + A would do.

7. At the bottom of the document back off (de-highlight) the last return. Now press Control C to copy, open up a new document and in the new document under inset use "**paste special** and choose **unformatted text**" which essentially strips it clean. Place the document on the system and style using firm styles.

8. As long as you have the time **strip and reformat** is a typical WP request.

........*

An Overview of Proofreading:

Operators and Proofreaders work very closely together when it comes to all the documents that come into the center. Anytime you do work on a document whether you start it from scratch or you do edits to an existing document you will always give the document over to proofreading after you complete the work.

The Proofreaders will look over your edits that you did on the behalf of the attorney and will make corrections as needed based on things that you missed. These proofreader corrections are known in the industry as **PC's.**

Types of Proofreading:

Full Read:

When a Proofreader receives a job that is a full read here is the situation. Most probably, a hard copy at some point was submitted to the center representing a document that was not yet on the system and needed to be scanned, styled, formatted and made to look like the submitted hard copy. Once it was styled and formatted, the proofreader would then look at the original hard copy as "the Master" and would go line by line checking the newly formatted printed out document against the Master and putting in PC's wherever needed so that the newly created file will eventually match the master after a few rounds of PC's.

Cold Read (Read through for sense no master):

In this scenario, a hard copy is submitted to the center. It makes no difference whether it is on the system or not. What they are asking the Proofreader to do is to take this document and simply read it line by line to see if they spot errors. When they find an error they flag it and after they have looked through the entire document, they hand the document back to the attorney with all of the flags on it for them to review.

Revisions

In this situation they are asking the Proofreader to just proofread the revisions that the WP Operator makes to the document on the mark-up submitted to the center. When the WP Operator submits the job to Proofreading after they have made the attorney edits, the proofreader concentrates solely on the revisions made to the document and not the entire document as in a Full Read.

Blackline (Caret and Score)

Full Read

Revisions Only

This is asking for an old style Blackline where the Proofreader will be asked to do a Full Read where there will be a Master and a Newly created copy that might have had revisions made as well to the document and anywhere that something does not appear in the Newer document that appears in the Master they will mark that area of the Newer document with a **Carrot** ^ symbol. Anything that appears in the Newer Document that does not appear in the Master will be marked with an underscore in the Newer document.

........*

Don't Forget the Page Number
From Portrait to Landscape to Portrait

This is not a major point but if I had a dollar for every time that a Landscape Financial Table or Chart or graph was placed in a document in landscape and then x number of copies needed to be made only to find the page numbering that was continued from the other section is now still in position on the Landscape page as it sits on the Portrait page thus being "way off center" on the Landscape page. If it is a draft that needed to be distributed then not such a big deal but if not, someone is certainly going to spot that and it will have to be corrected and copies if not for draft purposes, would need to be done over.

So with that being said:

1. You start off with Portrait and at some point there is for our example a very large financial table that needs to be inserted within the document. Now, you create a section break and then select Landscape for the Page Layout.

2. Many people rely on the center tab that is part of the footer for the positioning of the page numbering. This is the reason why the numbering does not auto adjust when switching from portrait to Landscape. The center tab is usually tugged into place (tugged to the right in the ruler) for the Landscape page number to appear centered.

3. I usually like to just use the center button and not the center tab. I just find it easier to deal with in terms of centering the page numbering in the footer. Either way, when you establish the Landscape page, make sure you center the page number and when you insert your next section break to go back to Portrait, make sure that the page numbering is centered properly on that page as well.

4. Important to note that in some situations, the attorney will instruct you not to make a Landscape page but to instead **stack the headings** so what they do with that large table is if the table has 12 columns they take the first 6 headings and the info involved and underneath that piece they take the **next 6 headings and the info underneath the remaining Columns and they stack it on top of each other** so that the

table exists within the Portrait format. In this way the whole document remains portrait.

........*

X Marks The Spot

Well, anyone working in a center has seen this happen.

Scenario: You set up labels for a mailing. They could be 2x4 or Return Address- 80 to a sheet.

It does not matter.

Let us say there are 250 recipients. The labels go in the printer and when they come out they look great! So, what's the problem?

They printed on the backside of the label sheets.

1. I cannot tell you how many times I have seen both operators as well as secretaries take the labels and dump them in the garbage.

2. It was an error but most of the time you can place those same label sheets back in the printer the opposite way from the first time and it will print out fine on the actual labels. When you use a quality laser printer like they use at most firms, there is no bleed through of the ink onto the labels from the opposite side so most of the time you can salvage them.

3. An old trick is to place an X on a blank sheet of paper and load that sheet in the printer face up. Put some text on your screen and send it to print. The X side represents the label side. This then tells you whether your labels on the printer you are using, go in **face up** or **face down**. Depending on the printer you are using, you may get different results from placing labels in the tray vs. placing the label sheets in the side feeder. So use the X routine to confirm both.

4. You may not think that this is such a big deal but labels are very expensive. You would be shocked at the amount of money that is spent in a typical firm for a mundane thing such as labels.

5. Finally, if you go to Avery.com they give you a free label template software which I have used for CD and Jewel Cases and many other projects involving labels whereby it is easy to use and gives you the ability to design labels from scratch.

6. It is important to note that if you just printed out 100 label sheets and you made the error where it printed on the back go to another printer before you run those same sheets through the proper way. The printer that you just used will be so hot that you run the risk of the labels pealing off onto the roller and then you have a bad problem. Go to a "**cold printer**" before you run out the next big batch.

Another MS Office Skill To Consider

Whether you are using 2007-10 Microsoft Publisher is another good program to examine and become comfortable with. 2003 Publisher was a very good program as well but they have integrated much more MS Word and Power Point Functionality into the Microsoft Publisher software.

As part of our training we have taught Microsoft Publisher to many students who have used the program in jobs where they function as an operator and a desktop publisher when called upon.

1. Publisher gives you a large choice of template selections for Brochures, Flyers, E-Mail Campaigns, Letter Heads, Envelopes and Business Cards.

2. It also allows you to create a matching set so if you create a brochure, then you can then do letterhead, envelopes, and business cards using the same design.

3. The program gives you a lot of ability for shading and tinting and all types of effects and color combinations that can be applied to your text boxes and other objects and shapes.

4. Yes we do have Vista Print, but to be able to produce high quality brochures and campaigns of all types, learn Microsoft Publisher and add another valuable software to your resume.

........*

Adobe Professional - Fillable Forms

In addition to an article I wrote last week, concerning learning Microsoft Publisher to add to your skill set another to consider is Fillable forms in Adobe Professional.

Using the Advance Editing Toolbar you can scan in any form no matter how intricate and even though it is only a picture, you can set it up rather easily to be able to just type in and fill out the form whenever needed.

1. You can set up those areas that need typing using the "**Text Field Tool**" and the **Check Box Tool** for boxes that need to be checked or X'd.

2. It will also give you the ability to do list boxes where a menu opens up and you pick a particular item from a set of choices.

3. Fillable forms are very simple to learn. We teach this all the time.

4. Learning Fillable forms gives those at the office one less thing to have to use the typewriter for. Also, by making a "template" like document after you finish

the Fillable form, you set the security so that you allow the file to be copied but not able to alter the original. This then gives you an inexhaustible supply of forms to use.

5. When you fill out the form, you can print the completed form or send the completed form by email to someone else.

6. Hey, if you don't have the money to buy the new Adobe Professional then go on EBay and Half.com and look for older versions of Adobe Professional. I feel that even if you can get your hands on Adobe Professional 5 or 6 you can still learn Fillable forms effectively. Someone may be selling the older version for $20-40 dollars. It is worth looking.

7. Yes, the newer versions look slightly different, but the menus are very similar and you will find that the older and newer versions will be very easy for you to navigate. Once you find the **Advance Editing Functions** you are good to go.

8. If you are industrious, you can contact small offices and ask if they would like their paper forms scanned in and set up for Fillable forms. Now is the time to learn and do as much as possible so keep learning.

........*

Thus Was It Written

This is something that I have seen happen on a number of occasions where a particular lack of knowledge was the cause.

An attorney submits a document for editing. There are quotes within the document. Within the quotes there are words spelled incorrectly. If that is the case:

1. Correcting those mistakes will only annoy the attorney.

2. Those mistakes (spelling errors) are meant to stay as they are since they were made by the author of the quote and need to remain unaltered.

3. **Important:** If such a mistake is made, next to the spelling error in the quote will be the term or should be the term [sic] which in Latin simply means "Thus it was written". While we are on the subject, if you see a set of single quotes within the quote that is because someone was being quoted within the quote.

Example: "I never personally saw Mr. Applehead be abusive to anyone, but when I spoake [Sic] to Timmy Timid, he said 'I have been yelled at many times by Mr. Applehead and he makes me nervous' otherwise I have always had a good relationship with him."

4. When it comes to the [Sic] correction, I have often been approached by a co-worker after the attorney tells them to put the quote back into its original condition complaining to me that they are not an attorney and therefore should not be

expected to have known that. Well, I feel that if you are in the industry you should know as much as possible and the more you know the better.

5. Any time you are working on a legal document and come across something you don't know, you should write it down and look it up when you have time. That will be 1 less thing that you can cross off your list of questions. Look it up yourself. The attorney most likely is not going to teach you law while others may be glad you are interested and gladly tell you the answer. You will know best who or who not to ask.

No one is born knowing all, but you need to continually seek knowledge especially in today's environment where the more knowledge you have the more valuable to the firm you become.

........*

The Useful F4 Key - Repeat As Needed

Personally it is one of my favorite shortcuts. I find it very useful. For instance:

1. I apply a body text style to a paragraph. The next 5 paragraphs need the same style applied. I could highlight the next five paragraphs and click on the style name in the right side "Styles" panel to apply a particular style to the 5 highlighted paragraphs or I could highlight the five paragraphs and hit the "F4" button in order to repeat the last action thus applying the body text style to those same 5 paragraphs. Either way it is up to you, but I tend to just go for the repeat key " **F4**".

2. Another example, I highlight the text of a Defined Term ("Defined Term") for the purpose of applying a "Bold" character style. I have another 30 to do. So I go to the next defined term and I highlight the text and press F4 which applies the character style. So I either highlight the text of the defined term if more than one word or double click to highlight the text of the defined term if one word and press F4 to apply.

3. Be inventive and use the F4 key to repeat the last function. Remember it is literally the last function that it will repeat. It is not to be confused with paste since paste does not care what you do, it just pastes the same text again and again.

Experiment with the F4 function to make less work for yourself.

........*

The Name is The Name:

This is the second time this issue has surfaced so let me just verbalize what should make sense to most secretarial and WP staff. This involves the name of Exhibits in the back of a document and the numbering system. Let us assume that the main part of the document is complete and the regular numbering system is in place. There are for this example 3 exhibits that make up the end of the document.

The first Exhibit is called Exhibit 1-1 the second Exhibit 1-2 and finally Exhibit 1-3. I have personally worked on large documents with 20 plus exhibits in the back.

1. Many operators just number the exhibit pages 1,2,3, and when the attorney tells them to redo it they have a look of redo what?

2. The names of the Exhibits have to be acknowledged within the numbering system and while some people could not care less, others want the numbering in a specific fashion. It is not the job of the secretary or WP Operator to dictate to the attorney how the numbering should be. A lot of the Exhibits are public documents that already have names and need to kept as is. The attorney himself would have to be willing or in a position to change the Exhibit names in order to accommodate your request for a simple Exhibit numbering system. It is not up to you to say well in the firm we only do this or we only do that. You have to be thinking on any given day that any given thing can be asked. So, let us agree that A-1, B-1, C-1 is very common albeit there are those situations where the norm is not in place.

3. When the attorney brings a document back to you to have the Exhibit numbering "fixed" they would like you to acknowledge the name of the Exhibit in the numbering system.

4. So, the first page of Exhibit 1-1 or 1.1 becomes Ex. 1-1-1, Ex. 1-1-2 etc. where the "**Ex. 1-1-** " is typed in manually and the final number (or actual page number) is using auto page numbering.

5. The first page of Exhibit 1-2 should read Ex. 1-2-1, Ex. 1-2-2 etc. where the "Ex. **1-2-**" is manually typed and the final number is using the automatic page numbering.

6. You may encounter this "once in a while" but you should now know how to handle it. Why do they do this? This is usually a large document. *If you print out a hard copy and pages get out of place, you don't want to have to guess what exhibit that page comes from and where you need to place it back into.* If all you are doing is plain numbering throughout the document and pages get mixed up getting them back in order is a lot easler if the Exhibit name is acknowledged in the numbering system. Then there is no doubt where it comes from.

Creating 2D Barcodes:

I am doing a re-post of this write-up that I did a couple of months ago for those who may have missed it. Many firms, law firms included, individuals, large and small businesses, are now including this technology on their business cards and packaging and boxes. Those people with the 2D Reader App on their phone can read the bar code which will direct them to the main website of the company or a specific location within the site or landing page. They are easy to create.

In the age of Smart Phones and iPad like devices you need to know and understand what this advertising tool is about and this write up

First there are many free QR 2D Free Barcode Generators. For the sake of this article let us use the site below but please do look up other free 2D Barcode Creators

Below is a free Barcode Generator site and I also gave you additional instructional material below in the attached PDF link that gives you a great overview and some strategy. Go into the site directly below and create your own 2D Barcode. Remember to select the "QR" type code and then you will be directed to place in the link info that will be embedded into the barcode. You then copy the code and apply it to a business card or CD Label or Envelope etc.

http://www.barcode-generator.org/

By the way, you can get the 2D Reader App from:

www.getscanlife.com. Microsoft Tag also requires you to download a free app, from http://gettag.mobi

Step 1 of 5

Launch your browser and navigate to a website that offers a free 2-D bar code generator tool, such as Kaywa QR-Code Generator, QRStuff or GoQR.

Step 2 of 5

Select the type of information you want to encode into your 2-D bar code using the radio buttons or tabs, depending on the generator tool you are using. For example, select whether you are encoding a URL, address book entry, email or SMS text message.

Step 3 of 5

Type the applicable information into the text boxes provided, using standard alphanumeric characters. If you are creating an address book entry, for example, enter your name in the "Name" box, your address in the "Address" boxes and your email address in the "Email" box. If you are encoding a Web link, enter the full website address in the "URL" box.

Step 4 of 5

Click the "Generate" button to create the 2-D bar code. This encoded matrix image will be displayed by the generator tool once encoding is complete.

Step 5 of 5

Right click the 2-D bar code image and select "Save As." Enter a name for the image and save it to your computer for future use.

Tips & Warnings

To encode a Web address that is very long, simplify the 2-D bar code by first using a URL-shortening service such as Bit.ly or Goo.gl, and encode the short URL instead.

When encoding an email, you can enter more than just the body text. You can also specify the sender, recipient and subject line, and encode them all into a single 2-D bar code image.

Put a 2-D bar code containing your contact details on your business cards, so recipients can scan your details directly into their cellphones or smartphones.

Complex 2-D bar codes containing a lot of text should be displayed in a large matrix image to ensure that bar code readers can capture an image of sufficient quality to decode the data.

http://www.csuci.edu/news/documents/2011-2dbarcodeinfo.pdf

........*

Quotes Some Facts:

We don't always talk about quotes but as a secretary or operator there are a few things you should know:

1. Well most "Block" quotes are pushed in an additional 0.5 on both sides

2. The end quote comes in after the period of the last sentence of the quoted material.

3. If your attorney is using straight quotes then use straight quotes throughout the document.

4. If your attorney is using smart quotes (sometimes referred to as curly quotes) then do so throughout the entire document. Don't mix because at some point they will catch it and have you correct it anyway.

5. Understand what interior quotes are: **Interior quotes** are quotes with quotes. Note that the interior quote is shown as an apostrophe like symbol before and after the interior quote as shown in the example below.

"When I first met him he specifically said 'I am an expert in the field of Rocket Science' so I took his word for it."

6.   If you want to wholesale change the Quotes from straight to smart (curly), or vice versa for the entire document, then go to File, Options, Proofing, Auto Correct Options.

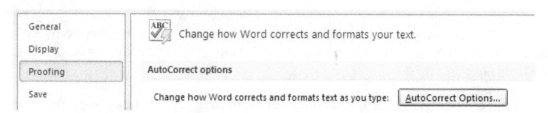

7.   In **Auto Correct Options**, look for two things inparticular. They are the **Auto Format** Tab and the **Auto Format While You Type** Tab.

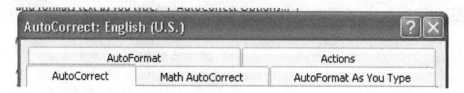

8.   If you want to go from "straight" to "curly" then make sure there is a check √ next to "**Straight Quotes**" with "**Smart Quotes**" under Auto Format. Then go into Auto Format As You Type and do the exact same thing. **Important:** If you wish to go from Smart to Straight quotes, you would simply make sure that there is **not** a check next to "**Straight quotes**" with "**Smart Quotes**" under **Auto Format** and **Auto Format As You Type**.

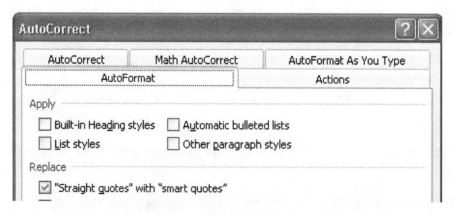

9.   The final step to change the Quotes from one style to another across the board, is to go into your **Find and Replace Dialog Box** (Control H) and simply place a quote in the **Find What** and **Replace What** area of the Dialog Box. The instructions that you set in the Auto Correct Options, (Auto Format and Auto Format As You Type)

will take over and do their job. Your document will now be uniform with straight quotes or smart quotes across the board.

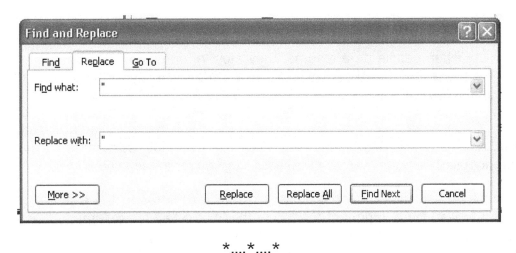

........*

The use of the Latin term [Sic] Thus was it written.

This comes in when within a quote there is a misspelling. Because the original quote has the error, if we are to use the quote, we cannot change the error but simply alert the reader of that fact so it would look like the example below:

"The reason that I quit my job was because my boss was thretaning [Sic] me."

Remember that quotes use their own body text style and are always offset on the left and right margin from the remainder of the general paragraphs so that they are easily identified visually.

........*

They Did Not See This Coming:

While this is fresh in my head, I wanted to let you what happened in this scenario. This will help anyone who is going for a position on any level.

A student of ours gets a call about a position that they were looking for. The hours and everything were perfect. They sent in their resume to the agency who in turn sent it to a WP Center person in the target firm.

1. The WP Center person rejects the resume and wants it re-sent because they want the MS Word version so that they can "**analyze**" how the person constructed the resume.

2. The agency person already had the MS Word version so they just emailed that off to the WP person.

3. The WP person then rejects a top prospect reason being that they felt their formatting capability was low and unacceptable for that firm.

Whaaaaaaat?

1. When people do a resume, they most often do so in a two column table. They put the text in and generally do not go overboard in styling all of the text in the two column table.

2. Because hard returns were used where soft returns should of/could have been, and certain letters or numbers were used without list numbering and styles were not used were just some of the reasons given for the rejection.

3. Personally, I think the content of the resume as to the experience of the candidate was more important than how they put a resume together. Most people are not thinking styles when they put their resume together. They are thinking content. The candidate had already passed an agency test with flying colors.

4. So with that being said, here is a mini lesson in the use of soft return and if any of you have questions just ask: The re-print assumes that a person is working in a center.

The important use of the Soft Return

When using styles for a **multi-line letterhead** or **inside address** or **side headings** or **top headings** in a resume, being in a center you can tell a lot about a persons overall knowledge by the way they go about dealing with multi line letterheads or the inside address of a standard letter.

If they create a style called for example "inside address" and the screen looks like as shown below, then it is not an efficient use of the style:

Letter·Head¶

Date¶

Style·name·inside·address·ABC·Company.·[Hard·Return].·¶
Style·name·inside·address·123·Maiden·Lane·[Hard·Return]·¶
Style·name·inside·address·Legal·Department.·[Hard·Return].·¶
Style·name·inside·address·New·York,·NY·10006·[Hard·Return]¶

The problem is that the operator did not make use of the soft return (shift+Enter) after each line of the inside address with the exception of the last line where the hard return is necessary for it holds the style information. Soft returns simply act as a line break but are not capable of holding any style information. So the same inside address would look like this if the soft return was utilized properly:

ABC Company. [Soft Return]. ↵
123 Maiden Lane [Soft Return] ↵
Legal Department. [Soft Return]. ↵
New York, NY 10006 [Hard Return]¶

Note that in **draft view**, your style tracking (left side) would show only **one instance** of the style name on the last line of the address opposed to **every line** as in the example shown first where a hard return was used on every line.

Some of you will be asking what does it matter? On the surface, it does not matter that much but....

1. If you are submitting formatted documents to the center or other firm offices in that condition you are advertising a lower level of understanding.

2. If you are taking an agency or law firm test, the person who marks your test will be looking for how you make use of styles and the efficiency of using them.

........*

Stacking In Tables

Scenario: You are given a financial table that is let us say 16 columns which includes side headings as well. The attorney has instructed you **not** to go Landscape but to deal with the table in portrait. In portrait, there is just so much room to deal with horizontally no matter what I do with the left and right margin.

I should also point out that the attorney has requested that we "**do not**" make the text so small that it becomes uncomfortable to read. Although that is relative, it is safe to say that he/she may not want to be looking at 6 or 7pt. font size. So, how do you deal with this?

1. I have witnessed operators spend hours trying to get the whole table horizontally on the page. When they are finished, you need a magnifying glass to see the numbers and the operator is sitting there exhausted and half blind as well.

2. There is another acceptable way to go about this:

3. What we do is to **stack the headings** so that with that large table has 16 columns they take from column 9 and place columns 9-16 underneath the first 8 columns including the headings above the columns. In this way, the whole document remains portrait and we can take advantage of a larger font. Some people will choose to repeat the side headings on the second set of columns just because it makes things easier to read.

4. Some people also offset slightly the second set of columns maybe by 0.5. but placing the second set directly underneath is fine.

First Set of Columns

Second set of Columns

5. This may not come up every day but this will come up sooner or later and you will have a strategy.

........*

A Term That Keeps Resurfacing

Anyone who has been in the business for any length of time would recognize this term. So here it goes:

1. Attorney comes into the WP Center and fills out a job sheet.

2. He/She writes: make a "**Supercopy**" and clean up the document. Make sure the document is using the firm styles and make it uniform throughout font included. Once the document is clean, create a new version and do the edits. When done, do a comparison, send me the clean and redline by email. Interoffice back to me my markup, and a hard copy of the blackline and clean document as well. Also, please make sure you update the footer to reflect the new document number. I don't want the old document altered in any way! Thank you. Arnold Billingtime, Esq.

3. Okay, so by now you guessed that Supercopy means dupe the document and create a new document number. Note that the attorney, Mr. Billingtime, also asked for a number of everyday Word Processing related routines. I count about 6 separate requests in that short write-up.

4. So, in sum, Supercopy an old Wang Word Processing Term is still alive and if you hear it, now you know what it refers to.

Any other old terms that are still hanging around?

........*

Style Separator Why and How:

What are we talking about here.

Scenario: You have a Multi-Level outline going. Let's say level one (Heading 1) is Article 1. and level 2 (Heading 2) of the outline is Section 1.1

Now, in many documents that use outlining, the headings are by themselves and do not share the regular paragraph. Sometimes they do, and when they do, the majority of the time it is the second level. It would look something like this:

Section 1.1 Provisions of the Contract. Text of the paragraph. Text of the paragraph. Text of the paragraph. Text of the paragraph. Text of the paragraph. Text of the paragraph. Text of the paragraph. Text of the paragraph.

Because the section shares the paragraph, if we do not put in the Style Separator, when we run the Table of Contents it will bring in the entire paragraph into the TOC.

So, how do we make sure that the Level 2 Heading info gets extracted **only** and not the entire paragraph?

1. Place your cursor after the period after the last word of the Heading 2. In the example above, it would be the period after the word contract.

2. Press your return key 1x. This will cause the remainder of the paragraph to fall underneath the current Heading 2 we are dealing with. Don't worry it will resolve in a moment.

3. Bring your cursor back up to the line where you just made your return.

4. Do **Control + ALT + Enter** which will insert the style separator and the remainder of the paragraph will go back in place to its original location. The style separator looks like a paragraph sign surrounded by a dotted box. ""

5. Highlight from the two spaces "**after**" the Style Separator and change that piece over to Body Text. Make sure you account for Justification and proper line spacing in the body text style used on the remainder of the paragraph. In fact, for the remainder of the paragraph name the style "**Remainder of Paragraph**". This will save you time of hunting through the different Body Text selections.

6. When you run the TOC, only the heading info of level 2 will be extracted into the TOC and NOT the entire paragraph.

Give it a try when you have this situation at work.

........*

Cross References

Cross References are one of those subjects that receive a lot of attention from employment agencies that deal with law firms. So Just What is a Cross Reference?

1. First you should know that a document that is going to take advantage of the Cross Reference function is one that for the most part uses the Multi-Level Outline Numbering feature. Most often, the references are found in the Heading 2 outline level of the document but they can also be found in the 3rd or 4th level.

2. Let us say we are in paragraph 1.3 of the document. And, suppose at the end of paragraph 1.3 it shows the following cross reference.

See Section 1.1 Appointment of Agent.

Here is the essence of why one would need to make use of the Cross Reference feature. Obviously, the author of the document (the attorney) wanted to bring attention and direct the reader of the document back to some point or issue that is going on in the Section 1.1 paragraph.

3. Now let us suppose that we did not use the Cross Referencing feature when we put in the "See Section 1.1 Appointment of Agent" but rather, we just typed it in. Also, let us suppose that the attorney comes over to you with new edits to add to the present document. Let's say that some of the inserts he/she gives you are new paragraphs that need to be added on top of our present paragraph 1.1

4. If I add 4 new paragraphs of material on top of the existing paragraph 1.1, when I am done inserting those 4 new paragraphs, my paragraph that presently says 1.1 will now say 1.5. This is so because of the 4 new paragraphs that are added to the Multi-Level outline numbering that keeps track of all paragraphs and numbers them accordingly. With me so far?

5. The paragraph in your document that that has the Cross Reference **See Section 1.1 Appointment of Agent still wants to direct the reader to the outline numbered paragraph "Appointment of Agent"** but it is no longer 1.1. In order to correctly direct the reader of the document you have to "manually" update that to say See Section 1.5 Appointment of Agent because of the additional "4" paragraphs that you had added on top of the original paragraph 1.1

6. So, what happens if you have numerous cross references throughout the document? Every time that you add or delete a paragraph, you would have to go through the entire document updating the cross references within, to make sure that they reflect the present outline number that is currently next to the paragraph being referenced to in the document.

7. In order for Cross Referencing to be helpful to us, we need the Cross Reference feature to keep track of where a paragraph that has been referenced moves to within the document due to any editing. Of course I am talking about

keeping track of a referenced paragraph in terms of the outline numbering system. We use the Cross Reference feature to keep track of a referenced paragraph after the adding and/or deleting of paragraphs due to editing. We need this feature to do this for us automatically so we don't have to do it manually.

8. So, if we have a Cross Reference and it presently says See Section 4.3 and because of editing, I had removed 2 paragraphs before the present 4.3 the Cross Referencing feature, after the removal of the two paragraphs, should now automatically update and say See Section 4.1, accounting for the fact that I had removed two paragraphs above the original location.

9. This is the essence of the job of the Cross Reference.

10. The easiest way to visualize it, is to say the Cross Reference Feature is constantly asking **what number is presently next to the paragraph that I am referencing and making sure that the outline number sitting next to the paragraph within the document "right now", matches the number of the paragraph your are referring to in the corresponding cross reference.** I recommend that you go back and re-read numbers 2 through 10 just to make sure you are comfortable with the concept. You find the Cross Referencing function under the "References" tab. When you do bring in a Cross Reference and you see the Grey shading, if you place your cursor on the Cross Reference number and do Control Click where you will be taken directly to Cross Reference of that paragraph.

........*

Friday staff at the Law Firm - Some Things To Think About

Premise:
It is Friday. WP staff has a long day ahead. People are thinking about the weekend. Chances are the weekend shift will receive the usual bombardment of varied tasks to take care of. Being that I spent many a weekend as a coordinator I can not tell you how many times a little bit of foresight could have prevented a lot of stress. Let us go over some of those things that would help to ensure a smooth weekend experience.

1. Someone should make it their business to make sure that the center has labels (2x4, 3 1/3 x 4, return address) CD labels, blank CD's, Jewel cases. Many a

weekend is spent doing Merge Jobs, Adobe Bookmarking Jobs and CD burning and Jewel case preparation jobs.

2. Are there clean workable head phones just in case tape cassettes or audio files come in that have to be typed (dictaphone jobs)

3. Are there interoffice envelopes and firm envelopes of at least 2 sizes to take care of packages that may need to be delivered to an outside party

4. Are there Federal Express and/or DHL forms and envelopes just in case packages have to be prepared for delivery and do those forms have the firm identification numbers already on them.

5. Is there extra reams of paper both 8 1/2 x 11 as well as 8 1/2 x 14 just in case a large printing job comes in.

6. Is there an easily accessible book of all attorneys in all offices or is it online and easy to get to. Are the car companies and firms ID codes for those companies available for attorneys who are present and need a car on the weekend. Are there conference call services that the firm uses and are they listed. If a call is to be held on the weekend does the weekend staff know about it?

7. Are there weekend conferences that will be occurring that the weekend WP staff should know about and do they need dedicated coverage? Any visiting attorneys and what office are they in.

8. Point being that many times many essentials are locked up and the weekend staff can't always get to certain areas of the firm that may be totally accessible during the week.

9. Not being able to complete a job for lack of supplies does not make the department look good. These things are avoidable and a weekly check should be done before the weekend shift kicks in. It will make for a more stress free and problem free weekend.

........*

Copying Track Changes From One Document to Another

When you work in a legal setting, the gamut of what you are asked to do is infinite. So, imagine you are in the course of a normal day and an attorney calls you or better yet, comes to you in person and asks for something that does not occur often but you need to know how to do it nevertheless.

So we come to one of these scenarios which is copying Track Changes from one document to another. Maybe the attorney needs to include a specific area of the track changes in a document to another. Maybe the attorney needs to include a specific area of track changes in a document from a specific attorney and display them in a different document for a multitude of reasons. Without this ability to copy track changes, you would have two other choices.

1, You could recreate the track changes in another document. That would be time consuming but you can do it.

2. You could snapshot the track changes in the source document and paste the picture into the target document or you could do the following

To keep your review/track changes in the new document do the following:

1. Save a copy of the Word document. [This is your backup]

2. Select the text you wish to copy

3. Press Control + F3. This will cut the text along with track changes. [That is why there is a need to make a backup of the original Word document].

4. Open up a new Word document or go to the existing target document.

5. Press Control + Shift + F3 and this will paste your selected text and your reviews/track changes along with it into the target document.

........*

II. Articles Relating To Working In As A Secretary In A Law Firm

Office Clicks:

Well, this is one subject I think everyone can identify with. You go to work and you want to do your job and leave each day knowing you did your best. I was talking to a student who was telling me about how the firm was divided into clicks of people who are not talking to other people and/or talking about people behind their backs. Clicks develop in my opinion usually because there is a general unhappy feeling within the firm due to policy, perceived inequity or people feeling stuck or unfulfilled and frustrated. A few thoughts on this matter.

1. Stay independent. Don't join a click. Reach out to everyone and be friendly to everyone.

2. Lead by example. Do your best each day and the rest will take care of itself.

3. Remember, you are not the job. You are an individual who does a certain job. Your identity should not be tied into your job. You are not stuck and through the course of your life you have the freedom to reinvent yourself as much as you need to in order to fit your current needs and situation.

4. Keep an open mind. Continue to learn and grow and listen for opportunity within your firm and outside your firm. Take an anything is possible attitude and every day will be a lot easier. Be open to all possibilities!

5. Be a leader not a follower. Don't join clicks. Realize that each job is nothing but a stepping stone and you will not be there forever. While you are at your present job make the best of it and leave your mark.

........*

Print Layout vs. Draft View

In Print Layout, you will see your headers and footers as you scroll through the document. In Draft View (Formerly Normal View), you will see your left side style tracking if your style area width is at the usual setting of 1 inch. In Print Layout, you will see text boxes and in Draft View you will not and so on.

Both views serve a purpose but this one little anomaly exists within the Draft and Print Layout View for which I don't know why but nevertheless it does.

So, here it is. You have a table and when you are in Draft View you can hover all day over a table but you won't get the little target on the **top left hand portion of the table** that allows you to grab the entire table with one click of the mouse. Instead you would probably go to table **select table**. You might select the table to then go to table properties to affect the table in entirety in many different ways such as: 1.) alignment, 2.) lines or no lines, 3.) font, 4.) before and after spacing or to remove the same, 5.) use or don't use **Automatically resize to fit contents** and many other reasons one might need to affect the table.

As soon as you switch over to **Print Layout view** and you place the cursor on the table, up pops the little **target on the upper left hand side** and the table is then available to be selected in **one click**.

........*

Modifying Styles: Two Quick Ways To Get There

Many of you are veterans of the Secretarial and Word Processing Center experience but many of you are just getting involved.

When we are talking about a style we are referring to a **group of attributes** (bold, single space, justified etc.) that are packaged, given a name and applied to text as needed. Depending on what the style contains, this will determine the effect it has on the piece of text it is applied to. So, when you are in need of modifying (changing the attributes of the package) a style you can take care of this in 2 easy ways.

1. Using the **Styles and Formatting Task Pane under the Home Tab (right side)**. Open the Styles and Formatting Task Pane on the right side and look for the style. When you find the style right click and select **Modify**.

2. A second method of modifying a style is when you are in **Normal** or **Draft view** (Draft View for Word 2007 and up), this involves using the style tracking on the left side of the screen. In this case, you **Double Click** on the Style needed to be modified and that places you directly in the Modify Menu. Remember the Motto - Double Click Left or Right Click Right to modify a style.

3. For those of you that don't make use of the "**Apply Style Menu**" (Control + Shift + S) why don't you try that method as well to **apply** a style. When the dialog box comes up you start to type the name of the needed style until it pops up to the top of the list and then you press return.

4. Keep in mind that these methods can be used when modifying Multi-Level Outline Numbering Documents as well.

Oh Say Can You See?

Returns, Spacing, Codes that is...

The importance of using Show/Hide

Well you most probably would not walk around the house in a pitch black setting. You would step on things, knock things over, break things, trip......you get the point.

So, when you are working on documents the show/hide button should always be turned on. This will allow you to see all of your on-screen graphics. I am referring to returns (whether empty or after a paragraph), soft returns (whether empty or after a line of text). Empty returns simply are returns (Hard or Soft) that are sitting by themselves creating a line of space but with no text on that line.

What about spaces between words? Do you want to guess or would not it make more sense to be able to see exactly what is going on with spacing. Maybe you only have one space after that period instead of two.

What about codes relating to Table of Authorities, Index of Terms, Table of Contents? With the Show/Hide off you might be accidentally deleting or typing over things that if your show/hide were on you now would steer clear of.

So when you operate with the Show/Hide on, you automatically are more aware and much more in control of everything going in the document you are working on.

Before You Pull Out of Your Parking Space:

I like to use this analogy when dealing with new students. It pertains to what things I like to have in place before I work on a document.

1. In Draft View (Normal view for 2003 and before) make sure that **Style Area Width** is **1 inch.** The style tracking task pane (which will show on the left hand side), will show you what style is applied to every piece of text. By **double clicking** on a style name on this panel we are in position to easily modify a style. **The Style Area Width control can be found under** File - Options - Advanced - Display.

2. **Field Shading:** should be set to **always.** This will ensure that auto numbering, footnotes, page numbers, TOC, TOA, Index of Terms and Cross References will all be grey when active. **This can be found under File - Options - Advanced - Show Document Content.**

3. **Right Side Style Task Pane** on the right should be open. With your right side we can edit, apply or create styles as needed. **This can be found under Home, Styles and click on the small box to the right to open the panel.**

4. **White Space Between Pages.** When in print layout, you will see Header and Footer material opposed to just a divider line between the pages. **This can be found under File Options - Display.**

5. Last but not least make sure that **Show All Formatting Marks** so that you can see all graphics such as tab, return and spaces between words. **This can be found under Format - Display**

Ready to go....
........*

Em Dash and En Dash and Hyphen
Distinguishing among the Three

This is one of those instances where you get the chance to add to your knowledge base. By doing so, at some point the newly acquired knowledge will come into play and you will be ready!

How many times during the course of my many years in a WP Center did I hear people say: "I am not an attorney, why do I need to know that?" Well, is there any honor in not wanting to know certain subject matter that comes down to the WP Center? The more that you are aware of what is going on, the more comfortable you are going to be and the better operator you will be. You should always be growing intellectually no matter what job you have. Besides, in this very competitive environment, take every opportunity you have to add to your knowledge. So with that being said, let's examine the Hyphen, the Em Dash and the En Dash.

The hyphen is the shortest of the three and is used most commonly to combine words (compounds such as "well-being" and "advanced-level," for example) and to separate numbers that are not inclusive (phone numbers and Social Security numbers, for example). On typewriter and computer keyboards, the hyphen appears on the bottom half of the key located on the top row between the "0" and the equals mark (=). In order to make sure that a hyphenated word does not separate meaning that one word stays at the end of a line and the other wraps around to the next line do **Control + Shift + Hyphen** when using hyphens. This is known as a hard hyphen or required hyphen. Anyway, it prevents a hyphenated word from splitting up.

Em Dash

The em dash is the mark of punctuation most of us think of when we hear the term "dash" in regard to a sentence. It is significantly longer than the hyphen. We use the em dash to create a strong break in the structure of a sentence. Em Dashes can be used in pairs like parentheses—that is, to enclose a word, or a phrase, or a clause—or they can be used alone to detach one end of a sentence from the main body. Dashes are particularly useful in a sentence that is long and complex or in one that has a number of commas within it.

En Dash

The en dash is slightly longer than the hyphen but not as long as the em dash. (It is, in fact, the width of a typesetter's letter "N," whereas the em dash is the width of the letter "M"—which is where they got their names from.) The en dash means, quite simply, "through." We use it most commonly to indicate inclusive dates and numbers: July 9–August 17; pp. 37–59.

In order to insert the em dash or en dash when you need it, you can simply go to Insert, Symbol and then click on Special Characters and make your choice.

Now that you know the difference practice using the proper one as the need arises.

........*

Multiple Ways To Use The Alt Key

And Table Trouble - A quick fix...

There are two things in particular that pop up again and again and can cause you trouble if you don't know what is causing the problem. These type of minor table related problems cause major wastes of time if the person going through them does not know the fix. Add to this someone waiting for the document while you are at a loss as to the fix, you have additional pressure of having to get it done. So, with that being said, let us eliminate these two for good:

1. You are using a Decimal Align tab and putting in a combination of numbers with commas (24,000) and decimal point numbers (32.4).

2. The numbers refuse to line up properly under each other. Although the choice of decimal align was correct in order to deal with the variety of number types, the problem is the alignment. Decimal Align will line up different types of numbers perfectly as long as the cells of the table are **left aligned**. Most often, the error here is that the operator or secretary has used right alignment.

Next, we move onto tallying up numbers vertically in a table.

Suppose you have 6 rows and for the sake of this article one column:

Row 1: 100,000
Row 2: 200,000
Row 3: No number
Row 4: 50,000
Row 5: 30,000
Row 6: sum of 80,000

1. Here we get a sum total of 80,000 when we add up the numbers when it should be 380,000

2. The problem is that in the row that currently has no number, there should be at the very least a "0" (zero) in that row. In this way, there will be no disruption in the auto sum function and your numbers will add up fine.

Knowing these two solutions will allow you to cross these two off of your "how do I fix this" list.

The Cool Alt Key:

Then we have the Alt Key: Using the Alt Key in Conjunction with the mouse. Go up to your ruler.

1. Press on the Alt Key and use your mouse to tug a tab on the ruler in micro movements.

2. Lines out of alignment in a table. Use the Alt Key and the mouse to tug the line back into alignment with micro movement control.

3. **Grabbing a vertical selection of text.** Here, press the Alt key and use the mouse to go straight down and across until you have highlighted the vertical piece of text to copy or delete. This is a great tool to literally shave off one line of text at a time going down vertically. Control Shift F8 is the equivalent of using the Alt and Left Click of the Mouse. It lets you go down vertically and across with the use of the cursor control keys.

........*

The Psychology of Email

We are in an age where everything we write when inside a firm is recorded digitally and stored on the firm servers for perpetuity.

Depending on the situation and our mood - this totally affects what is sent as an end result of what we were feeling. So, some tips from me on things you want to keep close to the surface each time you draft an email.

Scenario:

1. Something just happened where you feel you were wronged in some way. You immediately decide to respond. That initial email is going to show possible anger, insults, your thinking process, emotional issues that you have, insecurities that you have and will tell another person(s) more than you ever intended to reveal thus making you vulnerable.

2. That email was driven by emotion and triggers that are deeply seated within your make-up. Waiting at least a full hour before you look at the draft of that email is recommended by me. Never ever send an email out that results from an incident or circumstance that angered you.

3. Okay, it is an hour later. You have an email on your screen that is the result of where you were an hour ago. You have had the opportunity to calm down. First, we want to be factual in what we are saying and we want to strip out the anger, accusations, insults etc. and purely replace it with the set of facts, what has transpired and what you feel would help to remedy the situation. By removing the anger and other useless info, you also remove simultaneously the ammunition you could have provided to someone who may not have your best interest at heart.

4. By keeping an even tone and being level headed and factual, we remove the parent-child advantage that you are giving the recipient by not protesting to your "parent" regarding you being wronged. Instead, you are in an adult to adult exchange

and you are never giving the recipient unnecessary info pertaining to your emotions, what you may really think about them and what pushes your buttons and so forth.

5. Responding in a manner that shows confidence, understanding thoroughly the issues involved, making a clear and cohesive suggestion as to a plan of action is going to make people deal with you very differently than you loosing control. Also, most emails that are perceived as someone went over the edge are routinely Cc'd to many others while the intended recipient of a well constructed email will only be singing your praises if they decide to distribute it to a number of people.

6. Emails cannot be taken back and live on for all time as soon as you press that send button so keep what I said in mind and you will always look good.

Knowledge Is Forever

Below is a great quote from a Personal Development Trainer named Kevin Hogan.

"Carefully choose...who to listen to and the company you keep. If your mediocrity causes them comfort, your achieving will cause them great discomfort"

There are times at work where you may come across people who seem uncomfortable when good things seem to be happening for you.

It no longer feels like you are in the club. The misery loves company club. We are in an age where knowledge is either free or very affordable to obtain. I don't think there is one thing you can tell me about that if I want to, I can't find out an amazing amount of material relating to any particular subject and within hours or days have a comfortable working vocabulary.

I think when people feel uncomfortable for your success, they may feel that they do not have the same access or ability to learn what you have learned or access to the knowledge that you have acquired. That feeling of "maybe you can but I can't" makes people feel stuck and therefore uncomfortable.

It does not matter what you do for a living. If you make it your business to be in a constant mode of learning then you will surely be in a constant mode of growing. This is true for everyone **not** just for some lucky people.

What subjects have you looked into in the last week pertaining to work that you need to learn about? What books are you reading? If you have a sense of being able to do whatever you want to do, you will never feel bad or stuck because someone else has made a jump up the ladder or some good opportunity has occurred for them.

If you are bored with the current subject matter pertaining to your job, then look into things that interest you and start reading about them in detail. You never know where it can lead.

Tradepub.com has great industry related magazines that talk about the state of the art in hundreds of different areas of business. These are quality magazines that place up to the minute valuable information at your fingertips. So, whether you use this free site for MS Word related issues or not this is a great source.

Another fun source for quick knowledge in a multitude of areas is **howstuffworks.com**. Thousands of mini lessons and articles on anything you can think of.

Once you learn something, it is yours for good so make it your business to learn something each day. After a few weeks, look back at your newly acquired knowledge and I think you will be impressed at the ground you covered!

Are we at the end already? Well, I do sincerely hope that you gained much from this book. Keep in touch with us. There is much ahead. Feel free to contact us anytime with questions about our testing and supplemental material as well as questions concerning the industry and your career. We are always available to help. You can reach me at louis@advanceto.com or louisellman@gmail.com. You can also find my writings on legaltestready.com and lowcostempire.com

Always be looking ahead....

Louis.

DOCUMENT PRODUCTION CONTROL SHEET		Job #:

PLEASE COMPLETE THIS FORM IN ITS ENTIRETY

Attorney:	Atty #:	Ext.:
Client Name:	Client #:	Floor:
Matter Name:	Matter #:	**Return Instructions**
Document Title:		☐ Call when Ready
Date/Time Due:		☐ Hold in Center for Pickup (24 hour hold only)
Special Instructions:		☐ 15-Minute Pickup
		☐ E-Mail to:
		_____
		☐ Do not Print
		☐ Other: _____

WORD PROCESSING / PROOFREADING SERVICES

WORD PROCESSING	PROOFREADING SERVICES

Action
- ☐ Input/Scan
- ☐ Revise Current Version
- ☐ Create **New Version** under Same File Name and Revise
- ☐ Copy to New File Name and Revise
- ☐ Copy from Email and put on System
- ☐ Convert from _____ to _____

Program
- ☐ Word
- ☐ WordPerfect
- ☐ Powerpoint
- ☐ Excel
- ☐ Edgar
- ☐ Adobe Acrobat PDF

PROOFREADING SERVICES
- ☐ Full Read
- ☐ Cold Read (Read through for sense - no master)
- ☐ Revisions
- ☐ Blackline - caret and score
  - ☐ Full Read
  - ☐ Revisions Only
- ☐ Special Instructions (please specify): _____

Time Clocked Out

Deltaview/Compare

Additions	Deletions	List Versions:
☐ Bold/Double Underline	☐ Strikethrough	☐ Latest Two Versions
☐ Other	☐ Caret	Old Version _____
	☐ Other	New Version _____

Time Clocked In	I Γ H Γ E-Mail Γ Left Message with _____

System File Name:	For Word Processing Operators Only	N.B.
	Γ 1 Γ 2 Γ 3 Γ 4 Γ 5	Γ Return to Supervisor when done Γ See Supervisor for special instructions
	Was this job properly styled? Yes Γ No Γ	
	If no, was Attorney informed? Yes Γ No Γ	

FIRM 105067

Top Portion of the Control Sheet Explained

Job #: All WP centers keep a tally of all jobs that came in for that day. So, after the attorney fills out the Document Production Control Sheet, the coordinator places the next sequential job number up top on the form. That job number is part of the information that you will

Top Portion of the Control Sheet Explained

	place on your log sheet.
Attorney:	Attorney fills in his/her name.
Atty #:	In all major law firms, both attorneys and non-legal staff have an identifying number that identifies all employees who work in the firm individually.
Ext.:	Refers to the attorney internal extension of his phone number.
Client Name:	The attorney will sometimes write in the client name such as General Electric. All law firms have a corresponding Client Number to identify each individual client.
Client #:	The **Client Number** is the identifying number that when placed in the document summary portion of your Document Management System alerts the system as to **what company** will be billed for the work performed within that particular document number.
Matter Name:	While Client Name identifies the client, the matter name identifies the subject of the work being performed for that client. So while the Client Name may be General Electric the Matter Might be Lease of Facility
Matter No.:	Just as the Client Number identifies a particular client the Matter No. is an assigned number which identifies the nature of the work that was performed in a particular document for the attorney. So, when you as an operator are filling out the Document Summary of a new file, you always have to enter both the Client Number and the Matter Number so that the system that exists within the Document Management System knows exactly who to bill and the "Matter" to Bill for that particular document you were given to work on.
Document Title:	The attorney will sometimes put in a title that they wish for you to use on the Document Title Portion of the Document Summary of the Document Management system. **Ask us about our great DMS book that we have put together that examine a number of DMS systems**.
Date/Time Due:	The attorney will put down a due time on the job. Many times the attorney is going home so he simply says 09:00 A.M. Other times, the due time may not be realistic due to the amount of documents that lie ahead of his to be worked on. In that case, it is the coordinators job not yours to contact the attorney and negotiate for more time.

Top Portion of the Control Sheet Explained

Call When Ready:
If you are working the day shift, then when the job is done, the Coordinator will call the Secretary of the attorney and let him/her know that the document is ready for pick-up. If this is the evening shift, we can assume that the attorney is in the building and the Coordinator will be calling the attorney directly to let him know that the document is ready for pick-up.

Hold In Center For Pickup:
Here we can assume that the job was submitted sometime during the evening shift and the attorney went home. In the morning he/she will most probably make the WP Center their first stop whereby they will pick up their finished job from the night before which will be sitting in the **Outbox**.

15 Minute Pickup:
Some firms have a 15 minute pickup box. Meaning that during the course of the day when the mail room is open they make multiple sweeps on all floors to grab inter-office envelopes that need to be delivered within the firm and one of those stops is the WP Center where they will find finished documents in Inter-Office folders ready to go back to the attorney who brought in that particular document.

Email To:
This usually means that when the document is completed, that the attorney has requested that the finished product is emailed to him/her. They will then print it out at their location. In some cases, this is done as a backup since sometimes the finished document is in an Inter-Office Envelope and has not yet reached the attorney so it is just a way to make it convenient for him/her to open it up and look at it. Of course, they are going to want the Inter-Office envelope back as soon as possible because it will contain **their mark-up** as well as the **newly edited and printed** document and in many cases a black line printout as well.

Do Not Print:
In this case, the Coordinator will return the mark-up in an Inter-Office envelope or leave in the hold box for the attorney to come and pick it up. They will also leave an email or voicemail for the attorney to the effect that the job has been completed.

Final Note on Client Matter: The Client Matter number when placed in the document summary will produce a footer at the bottom left hand portion of the document that will serve to identify the document and allow for the operator, the attorney or his/her secretary easy access to return to that particular document. It would look something like the following example below:

NY1: 50043.1 10043/3342

So the typical identifying footer as shown above, starts off with a **Library identifier** which is this case is the **New York Office**, (Library Name denotes a specific server) followed by the actual document number that was created by the **Document Management system** being used. It should be pointed out that following the document number you will see a version number in the example above 50043.**1** which will come into play further on in this book. Working with **versions** is very important business when working in a Word Processing Center. Next, in the footer you see the **Client Number** and finally the **Matter No**. It should be noted that in order to use the copy machines, fax machines, getting a taxi home, getting supplies, will all need an Employee Number, a Client Number and a Matter Number. **In a law firm, everything is accounted for and billed to a particular entity.** For temporary employees, there are **temporary employee numbers** as well as general numbers that temps might use for certain situations but **no one is excluded** from having to place a client/matter number in a machine or a service within the firm.

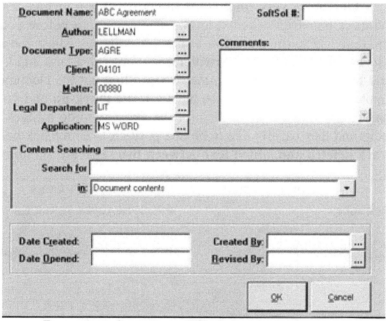

Document Summary Filled Out in Full
Clicking on any Ellipse's ⋯ will give you more information concerning each individual line

Just a quick note as it pertains to editing documents. Sometimes you will be given a rather large mark-up. You will usually (with a large mark-up) be asked to create a new version **BEFORE** you start the work. If you receive a large mark-up and **do not see that request for a new version on your Document Summary,** then, before you start, you may want to save a copy to your **"C"** drive, which will serve as a pristine copy. **What is the thinking here**?

1.   If they asked you to make a new version then technically if the new version is **version 3** your **version 2** will reflect **exactly how your document looked**

before you started so if something cataclysmic should happen, you always have version 2 to run to, in order to restore the document.

2.   If you **were not asked to** make new version and something cataclysmic happens then unless you made a copy to your "C" drive you don't have a pristine copy that you can run to. **Take Note:** If you save a copy to your C drive, before you start your edits **TOTALLY GET OUT OF THE DOCUMENT and go back in through your Document Management System.** If you don't do this, you may be **working on the C drive copy** without knowing. Then, without knowing, you will print the document out and hand it in. When an operator or secretary goes to the document on the Network **none of your changes will be in that copy but unbeknownst to every one, your changes will be on your C drive** and there will be mayhem. Most probably, they will make the center do the work from scratch all over again since they can't find the changes. So if you save a copy to the C drive get out and go right back in through your document management program.

3.   **One more very important thought**. If you receive a **very large mark-up**, and you **have not been asked to make a new version** before you start the edits, **I would bring that fact to the attention of the Coordinator** whose job it is **to "confirm" that the attorney does not want a new version** with such a large mark-up. The attorney simply **could have forgot** to mention that when filling out the Document Control Work Sheet. I emphasize this because if you have a **large mark-up** and you **do not make a new version**, it **takes away the ability** for the attorney to do a **black line** of the **latest round** of edits and they usually like to be in a position to do a black line which is **simply a way to track deleted and added text between two separate versions**.

WORD PROCESSING / PROOFREADING SERVICES		
WORD PROCESSING		**PROOFREADING SERVICES**
Action	**Program**	☐ Full Read
☐ Input/Scan	☐ Word	☐ Cold Read (Read through for sense - no master)
☐ Revise Current Version	☐ WordPerfect	
☐ Create **New Version** under Same File Name and Revise	☐ Powerpoint	☐ Revisions
☐ Copy to New File Name and Revise	☐ Excel	
	☐ Edgar	☐ Blackline - caret and score
☐ Copy from Email and put on System	☐ Adobe Acrobat PDF	☐ Full Read ☐ Revisions Only
☐ Convert from _____ to _____		☐ Special Instructions (please specify):

Time Clocked Out

Second Portion of the Control Sheet Explained

Input/Scan: Here there are a couple of possibilities. The attorney may have submitted a handwritten document that needs to be placed on the system from scratch. It is also possible that the attorney brought down a paper copy aka "**hard copy**" of a document he/she wishes to be placed on the system but presently it resides nowhere on the system. Therefore, we are in a position where we either have to **key** it in or **scan** the document using scanning software such as **Omni Page** and then style the document and clean it up until it matches the document that the attorney brought in.

Revise Current Version:

This refers to the version number of the document. So, if the attorney selects this option and your document number is **34536.2**, you will simply open up the document 34536 and the latest version .2 will come up. That is the version you will do your edits in. You will **not** create a **version 3**. You simply open up the document using your Document Management System and the latest version always comes up. Making a new version when you were not asked to, will anger most attorneys. **If this should happen**, bring it to the attention of the Coordinator and they can have the IT department delete the new version so you are back to square one and no harm done. **It should be noted** that if you discovered the error when you were already well into the edits, you can save a copy to your C Drive and let the IT Dept. delete the unwanted version. Then you can go into the **intended version** and replace that with the file you **just saved on your C drive** so that you don't lose all the time and effort you expended on doing the requested edits. You don't want to have to start over if you don't have to.

Create New Version Under the Same File Name and Revise

In this case, you open up the document and you immediately save the file as a **New Version** under that same document number and start doing your edits. The most common error in a center is starting a document you received **with a request for a new version** and forgetting to **Version Up** or **Bumping it up** before you start to do the edits. Everyone at some point has done this including myself. So, if you find that you **forgot to version up** save the document to your C drive. Now, you go to the coordinator and explain what happened and tell him/her that you saved what you worked on to the C drive. What we are hoping is that the IT Department can find an earlier version of the file before you edited it and restore that to the current version. Once it is restored you can now make your new version and replace what is currently in there with the one you saved to the C drive. You can go into the new version on the DMS and clean it out with **Control + A and Delete** then **Insert File** and choose the file from your C Drive that represents the document you did the work in. When it comes in, you are in your **new version** and you can continue doing your edits and *all is well*. In this way, all the effort that you already put in to doing the edits won't be wasted. You will not have to start again from scratch and most importantly the attorney did not know and the coordinator will at least give you credit for not allowing it to become an issue. **Be proactive**. Everyone makes mistakes and they will appreciate it that you brought it to their attention rather than an angry attorney. They most probably needed the new version because **they need to run a Black line** and present it to the client for review. That **Black line** will represent **all deletions and additions** that occurred between the two separate versions.

Copy to New File Name and Revise:

In this case you bring up the file **and save as a new document**. This will force **a brand new document summary page** to come up from **the Document Management System** in which you will need to fill in based on the info that the attorney placed on the Document Control Sheet. Once your new document has been created you **must check** the footer on the bottom to make sure that it has **updated with the New Document Number**.

READ CAREFULLY! A very common error is that this new footer information **does not get updated** on the brand new document. So, you or another operator accidentally go back into the document you were only supposed to copy and not edit!!. **Be aware!** This is something that will get you thrown out and again you will anger both attorney and Coordinator since the Coordinator will most probably take the brunt of the attorney anger resulting in you will never be called back to that firm. In fact, you most probably will be placed on the firm **DNU** list which is short for **Do Not Use.** Think about it. If the attorney opens up the supposed new document and finds none of the edits are in there but when he opens the one he told you **"only to copy"** he finds **all the edits in that document**, trust me he will not be a happy camper..

Copy from Email and Place on System:

This is another unique situation. They attorney has forwarded to the WP Center a document that is not on the Network System but he wishes you to place it on the system. We don't know where it comes from and we don't know what styles it contains or if there is corruption so hopefully we have the time to do the following:

1.   **Open the document and print it out**.. This will preserve the **look** of the document for formatting purposes.
2.   Go to the very top of the document (**Control Home**) *Do not do Control A. That will take the shell of the document and any corruption within.*
3.   **Press F8** (Turns on Extended Highlighting)
4.   **Press Control End** which takes you to the **end of the document and highlights the entire text**.. Back off the last return of the document and **copy** the **highlighted text** using **Control C**
5.   **Create a brand new document** on your Document Management System and when you enter the New Document, go to **Paste Special** and choose **unformatted text.** This will strip everything off the document and make it plain text and then you can style it from scratch using the firms' in-house styles.
It is important to note that if the attorney wants it immediately, then simply open the document and place it on the Document Management System, make sure the footer is updated with all the new internal document and client/matter info, print it out and get it to the attorney.

Sometimes, they want you to place a document on the system that has come from the outside, and style it from scratch meaning style it using the firm styles **after it has been stripped down. They then include** a healthy round of **edits for you to do.** Keep in mind that **many times** they will have you 1) place a document on the system 2) style it with the firm styles then 3) **when cleaned up and placed on the system** version up and then make edits. They are doing so because they want to be in the position to do

Second Portion of the Control Sheet Explained

a black line once you are done with the edits. So the clean-up is done in **Version 1** and the **new edits** in **Version 2**. Thus a black line can be performed.

Convert from ____ to _____

Here they may want you to convert from Adobe to MS Word and place on system or Convert from Word Perfect and place on system. In both cases, you may have to strip it down to bare bones and style it from scratch and then there may be edits to be done in a new version of that same file so just keep this in mind.

Programs:

The two I wish to talk about is **PDF** and **EDGAR**. PDF as you know is the Adobe Program and PDF refers to **Portable Document Format**.

Edgar is a shortcut for **Electronic Data Gathering and Retrieval** and refers to the Edgar system linked up with the Securities and Exchange Commission filings website. When attorneys bring in Edgar documents an operator in the center uses a special software to prepare the word document to adhere to the Edgar System and then the document is filed on behalf of the client. Most popular Edgar filings are 10K, 10Q, S3, F8 and many others but they are companies that are on the Stock Exchange and file documents for the public pertaining to the state of their earnings.

Proofreading Services:

Operators and Proofreaders work very closely together when it comes to all the documents that come into the center. Anytime you do work on a document **whether you start it from scratch** or **you do edits to an existing document** you will always give the document over to proofreading after you complete the work. The Proofreaders will look over your edits that you did on the behalf of the attorney and will make corrections as needed based on things that you missed. These corrections are known in the industry as **PC's**. **PC's** are an industry WP term for **Proofreader Corrections**. Now, after the proofreader finishes looking at a document and making his/her suggested changes, the Proofreader will return the document to either a PC's box which is nothing more than a plastic inbox looking item just for documents **that have been looked at by the**

Second Portion of the Control Sheet Explained

Proofreader and waiting to be fixed up or will give it back to the Coordinator directly. You will not always do the PC's on the job that you were just working on. The coordinator might have already assigned you another job so someone else will pick up the PC's, take care of them and re-submit the job back to the Proofreaders for one more look. When the Proofreaders write on the document **"Clean"** that means that all the suggested PC's have been made to the satisfaction of the Proofreader and the document is now deemed **complete** and ready to go back to the attorney. At this point, it is usually given directly to the Coordinator so that they can **Log It Out** on their system that keeps track of **all of the jobs of the day** and then route it back to the attorney by Inter-Office mail or by email as well.

Full Read:

When a Proofreader receives a job that is a **full read** here is the situation. Most probably, a hard copy at some point was submitted to the center representing a document that was **not yet on the system** and needed to be scanned, styled, formatted and made to look like the submitted hard copy. Once it was styled and formatted, the proofreader would then look at the original hard copy as "**the Master**" and would go line by line checking the newly formatted printed out document against the Master. They will make PC corrections wherever needed so that the newly created file will eventually match the master after a few rounds of PC's.

Cold Read (Read through for sense no master):

In this scenario, a hard copy is submitted to the center. It makes no difference whether it is on the system or not. What they are asking the Proofreader to do is to take this document and simply read it line by line to see if they spot errors. When they find an error they flag it and after they have looked through the entire document, they hand the document back to the attorney with all of the flags on it for them to review. **The word processing staff does not touch this document**. It is simply done to alert the attorney of imperfections in a document that may be on the firm's system or not.

Revisions:

In this situation they are asking the Proofreader to just proofread the revisions that the WP Operator makes to the document on the mark-up submitted to the center. When the WP Operator submits the job to Proofreading after they have made the attorney edits, the proofreader **concentrates solely on the revisions** made to the document and **not** the entire document as in a **Full Read.**

Black line (Caret and Score)
Full Read
Revisions Only

This is asking for an old style Black line where the Proofreader will if asked to, do a **Full Read** where there will be a **Master** and **a Newly created copy that might have had revisions to be made as well to the document. Anywhere** the proofreader finds text that appears in the **Master** but **not** in the Newer document, they will mark that area of the Newer document with a Carrot ^ symbol. Anything that appears in the Newer Document but **does not** appear in the Master will be marked with an **underscore** in the Newer document.

Revisions only means that there is a Master Document and a mark-up that was submitted to the Center that the WP Operator worked on and then submitted to the Proofreader. The Proofreader only has to look at the attorney edits and show things removed **with a carrot** at the location of deletion and show those things that were added with an **underscore**.

Deltaview/Compare		
Additions	Deletions	List Versions
☐ Bold/Double Underline	☐ Strikethrough	☐ Latest Two Versions
☐ Other	☐ Caret	Old Version _____
	☐ Other	New Version _____

Time Clocked In	I ☐ H ☐ E-Mail ☐ Left Message with _____		

System File Name:	For Word Processing Operators Only		N.B.
	☐ ☐ ☐ ☐ ☐ 1 2 3 4 5		☐ Return to Supervisor when done ☐ See Supervisor for special instructions
	Was this job properly styled? Yes ☐ No ☐		
	If no, was Attorney informed? Yes ☐ No ☐		

Final Portion of the Control Sheet Explained

Deltaview Compare:

Okay, we are at the final portion of the Word Processing Control Sheet. You are probably saying that I did not know there was so much to know about the control sheet. I basically used the control sheet in order to allow me to

Final Portion of the Control Sheet Explained

familiarize you with a lot of what goes in day to day operations in a top-tier law firm Word Processing Center. This particular section has to do with Deltaview (WorkShare) Compare which is the automatic black lining program that is used in most top-tier .law firms. **We have a great book on WorkShare so if you want it contact us**.

After the WP operator has edited the document and the Proofreaders have made **all of their PC's and it has been deemed "clean",** the Operator will sometimes be asked on the Document Control Sheet to run a Deltaview Black line which means the following: The Operator is going to use Deltaview to compare **two versions of the same document number (such as 32425.2 vs. 32425.3)** or **two separate documents against one another**. One of the documents will always be considered the **earlier version** and the other will be considered the **current version**. The earlier version is always loaded first. They are trying to show what has been deleted and what has been added **between the earlier and current version of the document.** The Standard Rendering Set (meaning **the standard look**) is the following. Those things that have been deleted will be shown in overstrike or strike thru (~~I have been deleted~~) and those things that have been added will be shown as double underscore. (<u>I have been added</u>). When preparing to run a Deltaview black line, it is important to note that you can load documents from the Document Management Program as well as you can load documents from the C: Drive. Or you can load a combination of the two. The earlier version can be from your C drive while the later version can be from the Document Management System. **Shift Click** on the folder to the right of the Earlier or Later version will get you to the **C drive** while clicking **by itself** on the Folder to the right will open up your Document Management System in order to select your needed document.

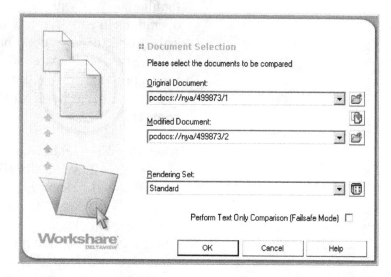

Additions:
Bold Double Underscore

If the attorney requests that the Additions be portrayed as **Bold Double Underscore**, I believe that the Standard Rendering Set will do that for you but if you need to, click on the icon **to the right of the Standard selection** and under Additions simply set it for **Bold and Double Underscore.**

Deletions:
Strikethrough
Caret

I believe that Standard Rendering Set will give you strikethrough for your deletions and if asked for Caret to show deletions then click on the icon to the right of the Standard selection and under **Deletions** simply set it for **Caret** ^ instead of ~~Strikethrough~~.

List Versions
Latest Two Versions
Old Version
New Version

If the attorney should choose **Latest two versions** then if the document has four versions you will be comparing **version 3 and version 4.** You would have done all of your latest editing in **version 4**. If he/she would like you to compare **two separate documents** then they will provide you with the two numbers and it could look like this:

Old Version NY1:343421.4
New Version NY1 667241.2

In this case you would most probably just did all of your editing in **NY1 667241.2**

Time Clocked In:

When the attorney fills out the form and hands it to the Coordinator, the Coordinator stamps the document under a Time Stamp Machine or other electronically related program and when the job is complete it is stamped as well.

I H E   Left Message with:

If the Attorney checks the **"I"** box then he is asking for his work to be Inter-Office mail service back to him.

If the Attorney checks the **"H"** box he is asking the Coordinator to Hold the Finished document in the center so he can come down and pick it up.

If the Attorney checks the **"E"** box then he wants the finished work to be emailed to him and the coordinator will also **Inter-Office the work back** to him/her.

Left message with, usually refers to who the **Operator** or **Coordinator** left a message to regarding the finished document. Unless it is a day shift where the secretary is the point of contact, the Operator or the Coordinator if leaving a message will always be calling the attorney extension and will leave a brief message. The message will state to the effect that the job is ready for pickup or the job has been emailed to you etc. etc. Each firm is different, but most of the time I believe the Coordinator will be making the call to the attorney concerning the finished product. If you need to make those calls and the attorney did not leave his extension on the Document Control Work Sheet there are **Firm Directory Sheets** in every WP Center that will give you that particular attorney's extension.   When it comes to inter-office envelopes if there are TWO ATTORNEYS WITH THE SAME NAME **make sure you distinguish them by middle initial** so that it **does not go** to the **unintended** attorney. This will cause the intended recipient **to be stressed** because he/she cannot find their mark up of the work they submitted so be careful and alert.